BITTERNESS

THE FORBIDDEN FRUIT IN RELATIONSHIPS

The Sweet Taste Of Freedom After The Hurt

SHAWN TURNER

DEDICATION

In loving memory and everlasting gratitude, this book is dedicated to my beloved Mother, Gladys Marie Turner, the beacon of strength and wisdom in my life. Her radiant example illuminated the path of love amidst adversity, steadfast commitment in the face of betrayal, and the transformative power of sacrificial forgiveness. May her legacy inspire readers as it has inspired me to navigate life's challenges with grace, resilience, and unwavering faith.

CONTENTS

PHASE 1

PHASE 2

PHASE 3

ACKNOWLEDGMENTS

I extend my deepest gratitude to all who contributed to the creation of this book, whether as supporters or challengers. Your diverse perspectives, whether for me or against me, have been instrumental in shaping this work. As Joseph's story in the Bible illustrates, what was intended for harm can ultimately lead to good. I thank every one of you for your role in shaping and molding me throughout this transformative journey. Your influence, both positive and challenging, has been integral not only to my personal growth but also to the development of this life-changing project for all who will read it.

PUBLICATION PAGE

Name:	Shawn Turner (Pastor/Author/Relationship Coach)
Church Website:	www.fhlccltd.com
Ministry Website:	www.shawnturnerministries.com
Book Titles:	"If Only I Knew Before I Said, I Do"
Book Purchase:	Amazon, Barnes & Noble and wherever books are sold
Book Purchase Link:	www.fhlccltd.com/store
eBook Title:	"How To Keep The Flames Burning"
Free Download:	www.shawnturnerministries.com/coaching
Social Media:	Facebook - https://www.facebook.com/sturner04 Instagram - https://www.instagram.com/FaithHopeLoveCC YouTube - https://www.youtube.com/@faith-hope-love-cc
Email:	pastor@shawnturnerministries.com sturner@fhlccltd.com

INTRODUCTION
IF YOU HAVE EVER BEEN HURT - THIS IS FOR YOU

Have you ever been hurt?

Is your heart broken into a million pieces right now?

Did a church let you down somehow?

Did your parents disown or abandon you?

Have you been mistreated?

Has your spouse dishonored your trust?

If you answered yes to any of these questions, you are in the right place at the right time to receive the breakthrough that this short, but powerful book contains.

This is a much-needed transparent teaching to help anyone and everyone who's dealing with trauma, hurt, and pain in their lives, not just to hear me but to listen to every word because it's going to free you from the deception the enemy has conjured up to literally kill you softly. I've been dealing with this for a long time but didn't quite know what it was until the Lord revealed it to me. Being a Pastor, teaching and preaching the Word of God for years, I thought I had a handle on this evil thing that has been developing in me for years unbeknownst to me because I thought I knew how to Overcome Life's Greatest Pains, which is the beginning stages of the forbidden fruit. This seed from the enemy is so deceptive that, like natural seeds, it doesn't produce immediately, but after some time, it produces the blade, then the ear, and then the full corn in the ear (Mark 4:28).

It's as subtle as a snake, but deadlier once bitten, and the venom runs through your veins to infect your entire being because it wasn't immediately sucked out or dealt with to stop it from contaminating your heart, the life organ in your body. Inwardly, it grows until it starts to sprout outwardly, which then begins to creep and spread within your relationships, family, and those close to you. It's worse than when we were inundated with the COVID-19 virus because most people didn't know they were infected and therefore misdiagnosed it as the flu or cold, which led to an overwhelming number of deaths that landed us in a pandemic that shut everything down. It was pandemonium! Bitterness has the same effects and is even worse because it can go undetected. It can be planted from the:

- Pains of childhood when your parents or siblings deeply hurt you.
- Pains from friends who betrayed, disappointed, bullied, and never supported you.
- Pains from employers that mistreated you, misused you and overlooked you.

- Pains from a spouse that cheated on you, abandoned you or even abused you.

The pain, agony, and brokenness that plants the seed of bitterness can come from anywhere. No one is exempt; it is not prejudice, and it definitely doesn't discriminate. You know it's there when you say you have "forgiven" the perpetrator, but whenever you think about it, someone mentions their name, or you are reminded of them, those feelings of hurt, betrayal, disappointment, and hatred arise. This can be detrimental because it's designed to slowly eat away at your life, and the next thing you know, you are old, angry, and alone because you have run everyone away. You see, one of the devil's main objectives is to isolate us so that we have no sound counsel but his deceptive counsel, which whispers words of negativity that play tricks on our minds to get us to follow his will instead of God's will. This is why it's so important to learn how to Overcome Life's Greatest Pains, which in due season birth bitterness to destroy you and every relationship you encounter and space you occupy.

The Lord has me writing on this subject because I've been hurt so much by so many people, even those who are really, really close to me, which made the pain even more severe. I speak from experience when I tell you that pain changes people - some become offensive, others become defensive, many become silent, while others exclude themselves, but I want to encourage you to become neither. If it doesn't kill you, allow it to make you stronger, wiser, and more determined to use it instead of it using you. Some of the most powerful stories ever told, movies ever directed, and songs ever sung derived from life's experiences of pain and hurt. If you refuse to listen to wise Godly counsel, you will stay on your back, your head will always be on a swivel, and you'll erect walls to keep others out, which makes for a lonely and non-purposeful life. Listen to what Jesus said when we find ourselves in this state of mind.

Matthew 11:28 ISV
"Come to me, all of you who are weary and loaded down with burdens, and I will give you rest.

Many people are burdened and restless as newborn babies with colic in the middle of the night, simply because their pride will not allow them to go to Jesus when they are in pain. This is not always the easiest thing to do when you feel you are always on the run. I do not wish this on my worst enemy, even though they are the ones that are bringing the pain, making me feel like I'm insane. We need to get to the point where our mindset is, "No Pain – No Gain," because pain and hurt are inevitable. If we don't learn to deal with it properly, it will slowly eat away at the constant dissipating time that is too short to waste on those who don't care enough not to hurt us. Never empower anyone to take away something they never gave you. So, as a servant of the Most-High God, He has instructed me to layout the natural maturation of any-thing planted that will unveil the different stages from when planted to harvested in hopes of catching it, uprooting it, and destroying it before it destroys you, your relationships and life as you know it.

CHAPTER 1

THE SEED OF BITTERNESS

To Overcome Life's Greatest Pains, we must first look at the seed that produces the root that cannot be seen that leads to the outward fruit of destruction. So, the first part of this much-needed book is the beginning process of this infectious disease that ruins relationships at an alarming rate - **The Seed of Bitterness.**

Ephesians 4:31 NET
You must put away all bitterness, anger, wrath, quarreling, and slanderous talk – indeed all malice.

Now, we all know a seed to be a flowering plant unit of reproduction, capable of developing into another such plant. To produce more of its kind, it must be planted in soil and nurtured. Likewise, the "Seed of Bitterness" is planted in the soil of our hearts from the pain that has been nurtured and protected instead of being properly dealt with and rejected.

This is why Paul didn't even play around with it by suggesting we should put away a selective amount of bitterness, which we may feel justified to hold on to, but he said we **"must"** put away **"all"** bitterness, anger, wrath, quarreling, slanderous talk, and **"all"** malice.

Are you bitter and angry with your spouse right now?

You don't have to answer me, but to have any chance at defeating bitterness, you must honestly answer this question for yourself. I have been married for over 28 years and plan to remain married for at least 100 more years. I know the math does not match but pretend it does and go along with me. The point I'm trying to make is according to today's standards, this has been a long time, but if the truth be told, it wasn't all peaches and cream; we've had our ups and downs. Marriage is hard and can bring about many challenges designed to make you stronger and become one, but if you don't know this it will do just the opposite by dividing you to remain separate. God's ultimate design for marriage is for the two to become one. Listen to what Jesus said in:

Mark 10:6-9 NKJV
But from the beginning of the creation, God 'MADE THEM MALE AND FEMALE.' 'FOR THIS REASON A MAN SHALL LEAVE HIS FATHER AND MOTHER AND BE JOINED TO HIS WIFE, AND THE TWO SHALL BECOME ONE FLESH'; so then they are no longer two, but one flesh. Therefore what God has joined together, let not man separate."

Making two people with two different personalities, beliefs, and upbringings into one is one of the hardest things you'll ever do when you get hitched because it requires you to become selfless instead of your naturally selfish state. As you can see, this is not easy, especially when you try to do it without God. However, when God revealed what I am about to reveal to you, it saved my marriage, and I promise that if you listen, not just hear me, and follow God's ways, it will save yours as well.

I have been counseling and coaching couples for over (20) twenty years now. Trust me when I tell you that I have heard and seen a lot of things that you probably couldn't imagine. However, one of the most common issues I deal with is distrust due to heartbreak, abandonment, and infidelity, which produces the forbidden fruit of bitterness.

The Greek meaning of bitterness is acridity, acid, or poisonous. If something is "bitter," it is generally translated to describe something that tastes sour or brackish, which is the polar opposite of sweet. It reminds me of when Moses and the children of Israel were in the desert for three days without water and came to Marah but could not drink the water because it was bitter. But God showed Moses a tree, and he cast it into the bitter waters, and instantly, the waters became sweet and drinkable (Exodus 15:22-25). Ironically, it was a tree and not a rock, stone, dirt, or anything else. It was a tree, which is the same element our Lord and Savior, Jesus Christ, was crucified on to turn our bitter waters of eternal damnation into sweet water of eternal life. After God turned their bitter waters sweet, He made an amazing promise never to put any of the diseases He put on the Egyptians if they would diligently listen, obey, and keep His commands and statutes. This is when He revealed another important name He goes by, which is Jehovah Rapha – The LORD who heals you (Exodus 15:26). He revealed His name, Jehovah Rapha, to them in the context of making the bitter waters sweet for them to drink. It's extremely interesting to me that the first miracle God performed, and the Israelites experienced after the BIG display of God's power as they crossed the Red Sea, was for Him to deal with the bitterness in the water. This was also an indication of His willingness and ability to deal with the bitterness in their souls resulting from 400 years in slavery. I know many of you can relate because you've been bitter for a long time due to abuse, mistreatment, exploitation, and oppression from others. Well, I have good news for you today: just like their freedom from bitterness was provided, your freedom from bitterness has also been provided at the cross where Jesus was raised high and stretched wide, and for you and me, He bled and died. It was at the cross, made of wood, where everything bitter in our lives was made sweet and usable for His glory. Only God can turn something sour, brackish, and bitter into something sweet and usable to sustain and strengthen us. To really understand the biblical meaning of bitterness, let's go back in scripture to look at the life of a great man of God, Joseph, the son of Jacob in:

Genesis 49:22-24 NKJV
"Joseph is a fruitful bough, A fruitful bough by a well; His branches run over the wall. The archers have bitterly grieved him, Shot at him, and hated him. But his bow remained in strength, And the arms of his hands were made strong By the hands of the Mighty God of Jacob (From there is the Shepherd, the Stone of Israel),

Jacob gathered all his boys and prophesied over them. When he got to Joseph, he had a lot to say because he was special. He was so special that his brothers treated him in a very bitter way; they took shots at him, and they even hated him because he was favored by man and God, who was with him and made him strong enough to endure all the attacks, hurt and pain that would normally cause bitterness. Joseph's story means a lot to me because back in 1996, I received a prophecy that I was a type of Joseph. The renowned and well-respected Prophet told me that I was like the black sheep of the family, and people were going to try to hurt me simply because of the favor of God in my life. At the time, I didn't quite know what he meant, but I understand it more now as I study his life and see how he was hated by his loved ones, betrayed by his friends or inmates, and lied on by Potiphar's wife, but despite it all, God's favor and blessings were with him because he never lost his faith in God. This encourages me to keep the faith and press on despite the pain, just like Joseph, because I know God is with me and what my enemies mean for my bad; God will turn it around and use it for my good, just like He did for Joseph. However, it's my responsibility not to allow the pain from betrayal to plant the seed of bitterness in my heart (Gen. 50:20).

The seed of bitterness is throughout the entire Bible, just like it is in our world. If we go a little further after the death of Jacob and his son, Joseph, who was used to save many people from destruction, including the ones that hurt him, we will see another account of the seed of bitterness planted in the lives of a people in:

Exodus 1:13-14 ESV
So they ruthlessly made the people of Israel work as slaves and made their lives bitter with hard service, in mortar and brick, and in all kinds of work in the field. In all their work, they ruthlessly made them work as slaves.

Saints, this sounds very similar to the history of slavery in America. The Egyptians forced the Israelites to work as slaves to build their empire, which made their lives very bitter with hard work and no pay. One race of people fought and even lost their lives to be superior to another race of people. God never intended it to be that way.

Galatians 3:28 NKJV
There is neither Jew nor Greek, there is neither slave nor free, there is neither male nor female; for you are all one in Christ Jesus.

People have a superiority complex that's not from God! This same ruthless mentality still exists today because the devil knows it produces the seed of bitterness that breeds social and racial divides throughout the world. It's a shame and embarrassing that we are the most powerful nation in the world. However, we are still dealing with segregation, degradation, economic inequality, racial divide, systemic racism, police brutality, and a host of other superiority unrest. We can defeat and conquer any foe but refuse to chop off the head of this disrespectful giant of injustice. It's important to know that bitterness is not something the Hebrews or the enslaved did; it's something they first experienced at the hands of the Egyptians or oppressors. Ignoring that reality, as we have done in this country, is not an antidote to sinful bitterness in the heart and life of the oppressed. In fact, it's an accelerant or steroid because it has gone for far too long without an apology, any form of reformation, or an ask for forgiveness that will destroy the bitterness, sour, brackish, and poisonous taste in the mouths and hearts of the oppressed people in this nation. The powers that be are trying their best, to ignore, hide, and not discuss the BIG ELEPHANT in the room that's taking up so much space that no one can move freely without stepping on toes. In the end, we are all God's children. The dehuman-ization of His creation needs to be properly addressed by first removing the bandage from the gaping gunshot wounds and replacing it with the prescribed care of the fruit of the Spirit of love to mend the broken hearts from all the suffering and mistreatment from the past to heal and move forward. Anything that we do not confront will not change! We will never be *"one Nation under God, indivisible, with liberty and justice for all,"* if we don't dig up this seed of bitterness that has been planted in the core of this nation from its inception and is still bearing evil fruit today.

At the end of the day, this is all a relationship problem. One ethnic group doesn't like another ethnic group for whatever reason, and because of the atrocities that have occurred and not properly dealt with, the seed of bitterness has been planted to produce eternal separation, which is the ultimate plan of Satan, the father of division. He knows that just as every kingdom divided against itself is destroyed, every household divided against itself will not and cannot stand (Matthew 12:25). Therefore, his main objective is to bring forth division in relationships to prevent them from growing together, which leads to segregation, discrimination, separation, and divorce, all caused from the seed of bitterness. Now that we know his game and end goal, it's up to us to stop it from working. So, if we truly want to deal with the seed of bitterness properly to prevent it from growing roots and fruits that will destroy any relationship, we must turn to the next chapter to discover the very first thing we must do.

Note: To go more in-depth about The Seed of Bitterness, please follow the link below to watch my YouTube video to learn how to pluck up the seed of bitterness before it can grow roots and become a stronghold in your life:

https://www.fhlccltd.com/videos
(Hover over Video Lessons and select "Seed of Bitterness")

(Please don't forget to Like, Follow, and Subscribe to my YouTube Channel and submit prayer requests on website)

CHAPTER 2

UNVEILING THE SHADOW: ACKNOWLEDGING BITTERNESS IN RELATIONSHIPS

T here is a very famous woman in the Bible named Naomi. You know the story where she left her hometown happy and full of joy with her husband and two sons due to a famine in the land. She found herself alone in a foreign country after her husband and two sons died, leaving her in the company of their wives named Orpah and Ruth. After the famine subsided, she opted to return to her hometown in Bethlehem, Judah, and her two daughters-in-law wanted to follow. To make a semi-long story short, Orpah returns to her hometown, but Ruth is loyal enough to follow her by any means necessary, no matter how hard Naomi tries to get her to turn away. Time passed, and they reached Bethlehem, where the people were excited to see Naomi, but due to all the bad that had happened to her, she responded:

Ruth 1:20-21 NKJV
But she said to them, "Do not call me Naomi; call me Mara,
for the Almighty has dealt very bitterly with me. I went out
full, and the LORD has brought me home again empty. Why
do you call me Naomi, since the LORD has testified against
me, and the Almighty has afflicted me?"

Obviously, she was hurt by her loss, and out of her ignorance,
she blamed God for it. She was so hurt that she changed her
name to Mara, which in Hebrew means bitter. Remember,
Marah was the name of the city Moses, and the children of
Israel came to in the desert with the bitter water God made
sweet and usable. The same happened to Naomi when her
latter became better than her former when she became very
instrumental in the union of her relative Boaz and Ruth,
who bore a son named Obed, which engrafted them in the
lineage of Jesus, the Son of God who came to heal the bro-
kenhearted. I believe the first stage of her breakthrough
came when she came out of the shadows to acknowledge her
bitterness. We witness the same type of acknowledgment
with Job in:

Job 10:1-3 NKJV
"My soul loathes my life; I will give free course to my com-
plaint; I will speak in the bitterness of my soul. I will say to
God, 'Do not condemn me; Show me why You contend with
me. Does it seem good to You that You should oppress, That
You should despise the work of Your hands, And smile on the
counsel of the wicked?

If you know the account of Job, you know that it wasn't God that afflicted Job; it was Satan (Job 1:6-12). It enlightens me how freely Job felt acknowledging his bitterness. Like most people who try to hide their bitterness, Job and Naomi reveal that we shouldn't hide it or pretend we are not hurt by what has happened to cause us to be bitter. They acknowledged the pain and how it had changed them to be frustrated due to what they believed to be unfair or undeserving treatment. Their freedom to acknowledge their bitterness is confirmation that it's okay and necessary for us to acknowledge the hurt and pain that has planted the seed of bitterness in our lives.

James 3:14 CEV
But if your heart is full of bitter jealousy and selfishness, don't brag or lie to cover up the truth.

We must acknowledge bitterness exists in our hearts and stop covering it up. The biggest deception the devil plays on humanity is to make them believe he doesn't exist. To defeat or improve anything, we must acknowledge that it exists. There is no way we can deny the very existence of bitterness. If you want to see the effects of bitterness, just look around. Bitterness is a terrible condition that will eat away at you, as rust eats through anything metallic if not treated properly. Bitterness is a reality that must be faced and not ignored, admitted and not concealed, acknowledged and not denied. I didn't just wake up one day and decide to be bitter. No, when I was hurt, the seed was planted, and because I didn't deal with it properly, it grew out of control. Being a Pastor, I thought how you deal with hurt was to ignore it, not face it, forgive, forget, and move on, but I was wrong. We have been taught for years that the Word of God says to rejoice in the Lord always, count it all joy when faced with trials, and give thanks to God in all things, which are all true. However, balance is the key to life! So, at the same time, we must use the same Word of God to learn to process the pain, hurt, trauma, abuse, and injustice that we incur throughout life. Otherwise, it will haunt, hurt, and hinder us from growing and moving forward in freedom and victory.

James 3:13 NKJV
Who is wise and understanding among you? Let him show by good conduct that his works are done in the meekness of wisdom.

Solomon tells us in Proverbs 4:7 that wisdom is the principal or first thing, and in all our getting, we must ensure that we understand. This tells me that wisdom and understanding are two different things, but they work together, as a husband and wife should, to gain substance. We define understanding as the ability to comprehend and grasp the true knowledge we possess. At the same time, wisdom takes the revelation of that knowledge and applies it in life to make the right decisions. So, simply put, understanding is the ability to comprehend knowledge, and wisdom is the application of that comprehension in everyday life. Another way to look at it is that understanding is the organization of knowledge, and wisdom is the fruit. So, if I understand something, I can apply it through wisdom to give birth to the right actions to produce the right results. However, if I do not understand something, I cannot apply the proper wisdom to yield the proper results. For instance, because I understand the damage of letting the sun go down on my anger causes to my relationship, I tend to confront the offense, gain an understanding, forgive, and move on to prevent the devil from having a place in my relationship (Ephesians 4:26-27). This is why we must understand what bitterness is and where it comes from, acknowledge its existence, and take the necessary steps to remove it.

In our relationships, we may get mistreated or mismanaged, which hurts us and plants the seed of bitterness unbeknownst to us. I'm not the one to tell you that you should get upset or feel a certain type of way when you get hurt. In all sincerity, it's good and appropriate to feel anger and disappointment when this happens. However, what is even more important is that we acknowledge how we feel and deal with it healthily through effective communication. If we don't deal with it promptly, it becomes the Incredible Hulk of resentment. When resentment, anger, and hatred are left to stew or fester, it turns into bitterness. Bitterness is something that many of us struggle with, but we have a hard time recognizing its existence in our lives and, therefore, can't acknowledge it. So, what I want to do is reveal at least (7) seven signs of bitterness to aid in your understanding to apply God's wisdom on how to handle it:

1. You have imaginary conversations.
2. You replay an experience over and over in your head.
3. You feel the need to tell someone what another person did to you.
4. You become easily offended by these individuals.

5. You have strong negative emotional reactions to things they say and do to you.
6. You can remember details of the things they said and did to you years ago.
7. You keep a list of offenses and can repeat them to justify your feelings.

If you can identify with any of these, you are most likely dealing with bitterness or at least the seed of bitterness that must be acknowledged to be uprooted before it produces a rotten harvest. I don't want you to be in denial that someone did you wrong. Otherwise, you may find yourself in the same position again. All I'm saying is it is helpful to acknowledge and remember that your bitterness is in response to real pain and hurt someone has done to you so that you can deal with it God's way, not the world's way.

The scriptures just revealed that true wisdom, knowledge, and understanding will be expressed in our actions. If how we respond is full of smoke, hurt, envy, and strife, it's the devil's or world's way, not God's wisdom or way of handling it. The characteristics of God's wisdom are found in this same chapter:

James 3:17 NKJV
But the wisdom that is from above is first pure, then peaceable, gentle, willing to yield, full of mercy and good fruits, without partiality and hypocrisy.

Remember, the wrath of man or eye for an eye or tooth for a tooth will never accomplish the righteousness of God. Therefore, we should be extremely careful how we react when we are mad or hurt, because those emotions aren't godly, and the decisions we make, motivated by them, won't be Godly either.

Romans 12:17-19 ISV
Do not pay anyone back evil for evil, but focus your thoughts on what is right in the sight of all people. If possible, so far as it depends on you, live in peace with all people. Do not take revenge, dear friends, but leave room for God's wrath. For it is written, "Vengeance belongs to me. I will pay them back, declares the Lord."

Many of us hold on to bitterness to 'do something' about what was done to us. We have been taught to get some 'get back' and not allow anyone to get away with doing us wrong. If you do not say something or do something, you are considered weak in most circles. But according to God, the meek *(power under control)* will inherit the earth and live in abundant peace (Psalm 37:11). So, don't be the one who wants justice and vengeance for what was done to you. Please understand that I get it because I was one of these people before God got a hold of me. I wanted to hurt the person that hurt me. I didn't want to wait and leave it to chance that they would get what they had coming to them. God said that He would prepare a table for us in the presence of our enemies (Psalm 23:5), which means they must be present to see what they meant for our evil; God turned it around for our good. We must trust the Lord because if we don't, we will remain in pain and entrapped even more in our Bermuda Triangle of feelings of anger, resentment, and bitterness, which is a terrible vicious cycle that is hard to escape and easy to get lost in. I feel myself breaking free as I am writing this right now.

So, here are a few steps that can be taken to uproot the seed of bitterness and break its vicious cycle:

- Acknowledge the truth that you are bitter.
- Ask God for His knowledge, understanding, and wisdom to handle it His way.
- If possible, effectively communicate with the person (spouse, parent, friend, etc.) that hurt you.
- Pull down the stronghold of negative thoughts and replace it with God's Word because as you think, so are you (Proverbs 23:7).
- If it remains and keeps coming up, pay close attention to what the bitterness is telling you, and then take action through Godly counseling and coaching.

Now, when you have done all that you can do, and it remains, you must not only acknowledge its existence, but you must acknowledge your inability to tackle it on your own. When you come to this realization, you must drop your pride, and clothe yourself in humility by giving your problems of bitterness to the Lord. If you want to learn how to do this effectively, let me encourage you to keep reading.

CHAPTER 3

DIVINE LIBERATION: CASTING BITTERNESS UPON GOD'S SHOULDERS

1 Peter 5:6-8 NKJV
Therefore humble yourselves under the mighty hand of God, that He may exalt you in due time, casting all your care upon Him, for He cares for you. Be sober (right mind), be vigilant (woke); because your adversary, the devil walks about like a roaring lion, seeking whom he may devour. (Parentheses are my additions)

We can defeat bitterness if we give it to God! It's a fact that we can't control what happens to us, but we can control how we react to it. We can't control people shooting bitter arrows at us, but we can stop the penetration. It's inevitable, but your significant other is going to do and say upsetting, unkind, condescending, and spiteful things to you; family members are going to say hurtful things; employers are going to do unfair things; this world is going to treat you in ways that will cause pain, hurt, and trauma, but we can't get bitter and complain, or we will remain. So, instead of grumbling and complaining about bitter circumstances or worse, ignoring their presence, God invites us to verbalize the offense in the safety of His presence because He is there to strengthen, help, and uphold us in our time of need.

God is our Father; therefore, we must humble ourselves and cast all our cares of hurt and pain on Him so that He can exalt us above them and the devil who is looking to use them to devour us. We must first be brutally honest with God about the bitter events of betrayal, dishonesty, deception, sexual abuse, disloyalty, envy, and jealousy in our lives. You might be questioning why we should do this when God already knows everything that has happened to us, and I agree with your sentiment. However, it's not to inform God of what happened; it's to release us from what happened and trust God to help us. We must let those sour and poisonous realities that the enemy meant to destroy us actually prepare us to find a new level of sweet trust and faith in God's power to heal us.

Never stoop down to the level of your offender. Try your very best not to get bitter but to get better. We must keep a level head because if we lose it, we just lost it - if you know what I mean. This is why Peter tells us to be sober or in our right mind. Being sober in the general sense means not being affected or influenced by alcohol; do not be drunk. The Greek means of uncertain affinity, that is to be discreet and watchful. So, we should ensure our relationship with God is intact so that we are always on the lookout for the enemy's wiles and schemes, not let our speech and actions go astray to give him access to our lives to devour us. If we are not sober, our tongues can release a deadly venom that will destroy our relationships and bury us even further into bitterness. So, not only are we advised to be sober, but because hurt, pain, and bitterness are so detrimental to any relationship, we must be vigilant, which is very similar to being sober but a little deeper. Being vigilant means keeping careful watch for possible dangers and difficulties. The Greek meaning is to keep awake and watchful. Satan never sleeps, so we must never sleep on his schemes because if we do, that's when he can come in and devour us. His aim from the beginning of time has been to divide and separate what God united – Adam and Eve. So, we are in constant spiritual warfare with the enemy of all relationships to try to stay together by resisting his constant magnetic pull of separation. This is why we must give or cast all our cares, hurts, and pains upon God because He is powerful enough to help and strengthen us to overcome them.

Please know that the enemy cannot just devour anyone, which means he cannot devour any relationship. Like a lion, he only gets the stragglers who drop out of the herd and are not sober and vigilant. He does not have the power to control people unless we give it to him by opening the door to bitterness. Jesus has already defeated him, and he is a toothless lion that only roars. It is through ignorance that we let the devil destroy us and our relationships. He cannot do anything to us without our consent and cooperation. So, as long as we are "in Christ," sober-minded and vigilant, Satan may try to touch us still, that weapon will not prosper (Isaiah 54:17). But when we stand in our might and allow the pain to seep in, too deep to water the seed of bitterness, it begins to grow, which weakens us to make us easier prey for him to devour.

I need everyone who is reading this to understand the importance of giving your bitterness to God. Bitterness is extremely dangerous and detrimental to you and your relationships. Harboring or holding on to bitterness is like drinking poison and hoping the person who hurt you dies. Please understand that the more you feed bitterness in your heart, the more it brings death to you, not the other person. It may feel good at first because you don't want to let them off the hook that easily, but what you're not realizing is it's worse than a venomous snake bite that kills you from the inside out. Satan is that snake and the poster child for the deceitfulness of sin. Whenever we love something that brings death to us, the devil has us right where he wants us because it cracks the door to allow him access to come in and devour whatever he wants.

Proverbs 17:9 CEV
You will keep your friends if you forgive them, but you will lose your friends if you keep talking about what they did wrong.

If we do not actively starve bitterness and give it to God, it will actively kill us internally and our relationships externally. We nourish bitterness by continually discussing the hurt, pain, and wrongs that someone has inflicted upon us. Now, I'm not saying you can't talk about it because I believe it's healthy to talk to your offender about what they did to allow them to make it right and not do it again. However, do not be deceived. When you not only talk to them about it, but others as well, and like all the time, you are feeding that bitterness in your heart, which is not going anywhere. There are three primary ways we do this:

1. We talk about the wrong to ourselves.

We replay the tape of the other person's offense repeatedly in our minds. This is perhaps the most common feeder of bitterness. Every time we replay someone's sin in our minds, we water the seed of bitterness in our hearts—and it grows.

2. We keep talking about the wrong to the offender.

This is when we never let the person who hurt us forget what they did to hurt us. We carry their offense around on us like a badge of honor. They are going to never forget what they did to us because we are not going to let them forget. Then, whenever any little thing happens, and we get into an argument, we bring up the offense and throw it in their face and rub it in. This is watering the seed of bitterness in our hearts, causing it to grow.

3. We keep talking about the wrongs of the offender to others.

Unbelievably, this is gossip, which is a casual or unconstrained conversation about other people. Gossip or constantly talking about someone and what they did is not good for the person speaking, the person being spoken of, and the person listening because their view of that person is now influenced, and it grieves the Holy Spirit.

Ephesians 4:29-32 NKJV
Let no corrupt word proceed out of your mouth, but what is good for necessary edification, that it may impart grace to the hearers. And do not grieve the Holy Spirit of God, by whom you were sealed for the day of redemption. Let all bitterness, wrath, anger, clamor, and evil speaking be put away from you, with all malice. And be kind to one another, tenderhearted, forgiving one another, even as God in Christ forgave you.

Every time we keep talking about a matter, we water and feed the seed of bitterness in our hearts. It's like when we have a soar on our body that starts to heal by developing a scab to protect it, but we keep picking the scab off, which prolongs the healing process and leaves an ugly scar. Every time we replay the offense in our minds or repeat the offense with our mouths, we nourish the seed of bitterness in our hearts—and it grows.

The Bible warns us of the danger of allowing bitterness to consume us, causing us to keep talking about:

- How it hurt us...
- The pain we are still experiencing...
- How awful the act was...
- How you can't believe what they did...

Honestly, I find myself getting caught up in this never-ending cycle with people who have hurt me, and my wife must drag me out of it because it's like I relive the tragedy of it all, which not only affects me but her as well. The Lord revealed to me what I was doing when I would constantly talk about it. He showed me that the reason I liked talking about it was because of my intent to vilify my offender and justify my sin of bitterness and unforgiveness to myself or others. Whenever we do this, instead of casting our cares upon God, we open the door for the enemy to come in to sow death-producing bitterness inside of us, which will destroy us and our relationships.

Hebrews 12:14-15 NKJV
Pursue peace with all people, and holiness, without which no one will see the Lord: looking carefully lest anyone fall short of the grace of God; lest any root of bitterness springing up cause trouble, and by this, many become defiled;

Ultimately, it is our responsibility to pursue peace with others, not wait for them to pursue peace with us. This is the problem in most marriages and relationships; one person waits for the other person to apologize or make things right. We waste so much time, which allows resentment and bitterness to grow. We are supposed to be a shining light of God's holiness and love flowing through us. If we don't act in a peaceful and holy manner, no one will see God in our lives. Bitterness causes trouble and defiles those affected by it. Again, it's poison. Please pay very close attention. Bitterness is a poison that, once taken, doesn't just hurt or poison us but also those around us. This is why we are called to walk in a manner that influences people in a positive way, not a negative, poisonous way. This is why it's so important to pluck up the seed of bitterness to prevent it from growing wild like the wildflowers on the side of the highways, which are unpredictable, unattainable, and uncontrollable.

We must give or cast our hurt, pains, and cares onto God. If we don't take action, no one else will do it for us. This is our lives to live. So, we must make a conscious decision to do the right thing to stop bitterness in its track. If we sincerely and truly want bitterness gone, we must be the ones to give it to God and then forgive, but that does not mean that we must necessarily forget the hurt and pain we experienced.

CHAPTER 4

FORGIVE, REMEMBER, THRIVE: THE ART OF FORGIVENESS WITHOUT FORGETFULNESS

The late and great Martin Luther King, Jr. once said, *"Forgiveness is not an occasional act; it is a constant attitude."* If anyone knew about forgiveness, it was him. I can see him marching for a cause and then put on pause when he gets arrested for exercising his constitutional right to speak and express his beliefs of equality for all mankind. Sitting there in a looming dark closed wall jail cell reflecting on what just happened, fighting back the tears of frustration and the desire to hate when he hears the voice of Jesus teaching his disciples to pray, "...forgive us our debts, As we forgive our debtors..." We know that he forgave because of his actions. However, we can also see that he didn't necessarily forget because of his actions driven by his pain and the pain of others to continue preaching, teaching, praying, and marching by faith, not by sight. For his dream to come to pass, he had to learn the art of forgiving without forgetting to thrive.

Matthew 18:21-22 NKJV
Then Peter came to Him and said, "Lord, how often shall my brother sin against me, and I forgive him? Up to seven times?" Jesus said to him, "I do not say to you, up to seven times, but up to seventy times seven.

Forgiveness is not something we do once and never have to do it again. Jesus had to forgive over and over and over again. His forgiveness is never-ending and always giving, even to this day. As flawed human beings, we are going to mess up and hurt people, and people are going to hurt us; it's inevitable. For this reason, I think this is such a profound statement probably derived from the teachings of Jesus, when Peter, His disciple who was always offending someone and most likely always getting offended, thought that he should forgive someone who sinned against him only up to seven times. This was a joke compared to Jesus' response, *"I do not say to you, up to seven times, but up to seventy times seven."* This truly magnifies the importance of forgiveness to Jesus and should also magnify its importance to us as well. Jesus told him like He's telling us today, that if someone sins against us, forgiving them (7) seven times is not enough, but we need to forgive them (70) seventy times (7) seven, which is equivalent to (490) four hundred and ninety times [70 x 7 = 490 Times]. Please understand that this is (70) seventy times the amount Peter thought, which makes it (70) times more important for us to do than we probably think we should do. Jesus knew people could offend others so many times in one day that He gave us an astronomical number to forgive.

When was the last time someone offended or sinned against you (490) four hundred and ninety times in one day?

Well, I'm not talking to married couples right now because your spouse has the ability, talent, and determination to do it and some. No, I'm just kidding, but for real. I used to think forgiving someone once was good enough. I used to think that just forgiving them was good enough before God revealed this truth in scripture to me that set me free. I can remember a married couple that was together for over fifty years that lived through multiple jaw-dropping, jail-worthy, and journalistic unforgiving non-jovial experiences that should have landed them in divorce court the majority of their relationship, but because they understood what true forgiveness was, they endured the trauma and stayed committed to their vows to love, honor, and cherish each other always, until death do they parted.

Matthew 5:43-44 NKJV
"You have heard that it was said, 'YOU SHALL LOVE YOUR NEIGHBOR and hate your enemy.' But I say to you, love your enemies, bless those who curse you, do good to those who hate you, and pray for those who spitefully use you and persecute you,

We are called to love, which encompasses so much, including forgiveness. I believe we think God commands us to do things for the sake of the other person, but in all reality, God commands us to do things that are beneficial for us also. Forgiveness is not to free the other person, but to free you, the forgiver! Those who offend us often remain unaware of the offense they've caused, and consequently, they may never seek forgiveness. We must forgive even when they don't ask for forgiveness for our sake, not theirs. One reason I honestly believe Jesus told us to forgive our offenders (490) four hundred and nighty times was because we can actually rethink and recount the offense in our heads hundreds of times in a day. We must forgive them every time they hurt us. This tells me that we can forgive, but may not ever forget, which is not always a bad thing. Thomas Szasz once said:

"The stupid neither forgive nor forget; the naïve forgive and forget; the wise forgive but do not forget."

Although we are supposed to forgive, there's a humungous misconception that the Bible teaches us that we also need to forget. The popular phrase for us to "forgive and forget" is not found in the Bible, although God did it for us as part of the new covenant through Jesus, who paid the price for all our sins.

Hebrews 8:12 NKJV
FOR I WILL BE MERCIFUL TO THEIR UNRIGHTEOUS-
NESS, AND THEIR SINS AND THEIR LAWLESS DEEDS I
WILL REMEMBER NO MORE."

God's ability to forgive and forget is what makes Him our Omniscient or All-Knowing and All-Seeing God. Remember, His ways are above our ways, and His thoughts are above our thoughts, so He is wise enough to do this (Isaiah 55:8). The last I checked, forgiving is not synonymous with forgetting in His commandments to us. Forgiving someone does not mean that we ignore what happened and how it hurt us; that would be unwise. Paul Boose said something that stuck with me, and I'll never forget:

> *"Forgiveness does not change the past,*
> *but it does enlarge the future."*

I recall one day, my wife wanted some tea, but she had an urgent meeting fast approaching, which stripped her of the necessary time she needed to heat the water in the kettle. Instead, she put some water in a cup and heated it in the microwave. Unbeknownst to her, when she reached to remove it, the handle was so hot that it burned her fingers. The excruciating pain she experienced burned that memory in her head never to forget the pain and reminding her never to do that again. I liken this unenjoyable experience to how we are to forgive, but not necessarily forget. We are called to forgive but not to forget, or we will get hurt again. Remember, forgiving changes one's perspective, but forgetting loses the lesson.

Forgiving does not mean we wholeheartedly restore trust because that would be unwise. I can't find where we are asked to forget painful experiences in the Bible, since remembering the pain will prevent us from making the same mistake. I used to buy into the belief that we should forgive and forget, but I found myself unable to forget those things that hurt and traumatized me. I remember being so hurt and traumatized when I was overlooked for promotions at my jobs several times. Still, it taught me to become so good and valuable to the company that they overlook the outer to get to the inner riches of knowledge, understanding, and wisdom to produce over and above expectations. So, I forgave the offenders on every occasion, but I never forget the uncomfortable feeling, which propelled me to become three times as good as the next person.

If we just stop and think about what trauma really and truly is, we will realize that it's not something easily forgotten, or it wouldn't be traumatic. Trauma results from exposure to an incident or series of emotionally disturbing events (rape, incest, molestation, adultery, abandonment, abuse) or life-threatening with lasting adverse effects on an individual. Many people are walking around oblivious to the fact that they are having so many problems in their lives because they are dealing with spiritual PTSD - Posttraumatic stress disorder or Posttraumatic Spiritual Disease. This is why I say bitterness is a disease, disorder, or condition and why the hurt, pain, and trauma that caused it should not be ignored, pushed to the back of your mind and forgotten. I liken bitterness to carbon dioxide, which is unnoticeable and undetectable to us, but when we breathe it for a certain period, it brings forth ill symptoms and eventually death if not addressed. This is why God never wants His people to forget or ignore the bitter circumstances that may lead to enslavement and even death. Instead, He shows and teaches us how to face it to make us better.

Revelation 12:11 NKJV
And they overcame him by the blood of the Lamb and by the word of their testimony, and they did not love their lives to the death.

We can't be delivered by the words of our testimonies if we don't remember the test that gave us the testimony. Joseph didn't forget the tests, trials, and trauma his brothers took him through; he just remembered more of the favor, grace, and power God showed him to get him through. He overcame his greatest pains to become one of God's greatest servants. We must humble ourselves to admit our inability to handle life's trauma on our own and turn to Jesus Christ with honesty and repentance to allow our bitterness to become sweet. Once we decide to acknowledge bitterness, and then cast our cares on the Lord to usher us into forgiving, not forgetting, that is a great step toward healing the wounds caused by the offense.

We know when the wounds and scars are healed, and the seeds of bitterness are no longer in our hearts when we remember the offense, and it doesn't hurt us anymore. When we remember the offense and don't want that person dead, hurt, or punished anymore, we are healed, and the seed of bitterness is plucked up. So, remembering or not forgetting is like a meat thermometer that's used to test the correct temperature of the meat for consumption. Therefore, remembering the offense and not getting upset can be used as a measuring tool to check your level of healing and spiritual maturity. We need to get where Jesus was when He prayed in Luke 23:34, *"Father, forgive them, for they do not know what they do."*

Have you spiritually matured to this point where you can forgive, not forget, but still pray for your offenders?

Or, are you still smitten with spiritual PTSD that will not allow you to forgive, and forget enough to put it away to where it doesn't send you back to when it first happened?

Regardless of your responses to these questions, your objective should always be to rid yourself of bitterness and its lingering effects. And, if the offense happens in a relationship such as a marriage, family, or friendship that requires restoration to move forward, there is a four-phase process that can help you reestablish the trust to restore your relationship properly.

1. **Forgive:** We must all forgive or release the offender of their offense toward us as the Father has forgiven or released our offenses toward Him through Jesus.

2. **Reconcile, Not Forget:** Remember in order to settle the wrong done to agree on its negative effects to bring forth change in hopes of preventing it from happening again.

3. **Repentance:** Evidence of change that shows a sincerity of sorrow for hurting you and the desire to do whatever it takes to reestablish and improve the relationship.

4. **Restoration:** Process of time to heal, build rapport to regain trust in order to restore the relationship to its prior state, and even better.

No matter the relationship, forgiving and not forgetting can be challenging, but not impossible. If you find it challenging, join me on this journey to discover the tools I've received from God to mend the brokenness in my life and assist others in doing the same.

CHAPTER 5

BANISHING THE BITTERNESS: STRATEGIES TO PUT IT AWAY FOR GOOD

Ephesians 4:31-32 NET
You must put away all bitterness, anger, wrath, quarreling, and slanderous talk – indeed all malice.
Instead, be kind to one another, compassionate, forgiving one another, just as God in Christ also forgave you.

Many people are spending thousands of dollars talking to their therapist about their problems, not realizing the root of it stems from the seed of bitterness. We become so good at dealing with the outward issues or fruit without dealing with the inward issues or the root, to only find after some time the fruit or outward issues reappear because the root or inward issues never disappeared. After all, we never "put it away."

We must learn to strategically banish bitterness by putting it away for good. It has been said, *"Most adult problems stem from unresolved childhood issues."* I didn't know I was bitter and probably wouldn't have admitted it if I had known it. I'm not the only one! Many people can be diagnosed as bitter, but they will not admit it because they feel justified in feeling how they feel. They may say things like:

- I didn't do anything to deserve to be hurt like this.
- It wasn't fair that they did this to me.
- I didn't ask to be put in this situation.

Pain is the catalyst that plants the seed of bitterness, but when we start thinking, saying, and feeling this way, we begin to nourish and water that seed that will eventually grow bigger and out of control. People say they want to be healed from the pain, but as long as they don't put it away by talking about it, they will never realize their healing. Paul said in our foundational scripture that we must put away "all" bitterness.

If we don't put away all bitterness, which is a silent sin, it will continue to break up marriages, friendships, and relationships, and hinder many people from finding peace and rest in their lives. Again, don't be deceived! Bitterness can go undetected for years because it starts as a little seed planted by hurt that grows into division, anger, accusations, wrath, quarreling, and even hatred. Now, I would be lying if I said it was easy to deal with, but I can say it's easier to deal with it as a little seed than it is as a big root or a gigantic fruit. So, when we are hurt, which is inevitable, we must acknowledge the pain and the seed of bitterness planted, immediately give it to God, forgive the offender, and then put it away. We must swallow our pride and instead go the way of humility as Jesus did, who suffered traumatic events of being betrayed, denied, whipped, mocked, pierced, and even brought to tears because they didn't believe, and yet and still, He never allowed the seed of bitterness to steal the greatness God placed in Him to fulfill. He acknowledged, gave, forgave, and put it all away to stay the course to bring us our freedom to live an abundant life to do the same. He is our example of how to walk through the fire and not get burned or even smell like smoke. So, keep your mind and eyes on Him to love as He loved despite what was done to Him, and you'll be able to run your race as He did by the power of God.

Colossians 3:2 ESV
Set your mind on things that are above, not on things that are on earth.

It has been proven that it's impossible to think about two things at the same time. That's why if you are hurting in one area of your body and you cause pain in another area of your body, your brain automatically focuses on the most severe pains. So, to starve our souls of one thing, we must feed our souls with something else. The most powerful force we have on this earth is love, which never fails and always prevails.

1 John 4:19-21 NKJV
We love Him because He first loved us. If someone says, "I love God," and hates his brother, he is a liar; for he who does not love his brother whom he has seen, how can he love God whom he has not seen? And this commandment we have from Him: that he who loves God must love his brother also.

This is a very profound and powerful truth that we must never forget. God never asks us to do something that He has not done or is willing to do first. He never asked us to love Him first; then He'll love us like this world has conditioned us to "love." God loved us first, while we were still caught up in our sins and completely unlovable. He can do this because He is God, and God is love. Think about it: God had to love the same people who hated Him, despised Him, and crucified His Only Begotten Son, Jesus. Love puts away offenses to pick up the offender to show them the right way. Love bears all, believes all, hopes all, and endures all things, which makes it impossible to fail (1 Corinthians 13:7-8). If this isn't love, I don't know what is.

Romans 5:8 NKJV
But God demonstrates His own love toward us in that while we were still sinners, Christ died for us.

Please understand that love begets love. It's because of His unsolicited voluntary love for us first that we can love Him. So, holiness isn't necessary for a relationship with our Holy God but rather a result of a relationship with our Holy God. If God doesn't require us to be holy, perfect, and without blame to have a relationship, why should we? Now, I am not saying that we must be fools to let people do us wrong, and we just put up with their foolishness. However, if they do us wrong, we don't have to stay mad at them or hold grudges against them. We can thank God for revealing who they are and allowing us to deal with them according to who they are and not who they pretend to be. At my age, I view it as a blessing because now I don't have to waste time trying to figure out who they are. So, if someone shows you who they are, believe them to save yourself a lot of future heartache and pain. Listen to what Maya Angelou once said:

> *"When someone shows you who they are, believe them the first time. People know themselves much better than you do. That's why it's important to stop expecting them to be something other than who they are."*

Now, don't misunderstand me to say that we must stop loving them. Love is an action word that overrides how we feel. We determine our love for God by our actions toward His children. If we say we love God, but hate people whom God loves, we are liars according to the 1 John 4:20 scripture we just read. Relationship with the Lord will cause us to have a loving relationship with His people. This is one of the greatest indications of our relationship with the Lord. So, being able to put away bitterness and not allow it to infect the wounds of the hurt exemplifies our relationship with God, who was able to "put away" all offenses toward Him because of His love for us.

So, one effective way God has shown me to "put away" bitterness is by preoccupying ourselves with His love toward us. If anyone has the right to be bitter at anyone, God does, but He chooses not to because of love. Nothing can separate us from His love (Romans 8:35). Therefore, rehearsing God's love, grace, and mercy, not justice, toward us is always the first step in starving bitterness and cultivating forgiveness toward others, which is the second effective way I know of to "put away" bitterness.

We've discussed the importance of forgiveness in the last chapter, but I believe it's important to mention it again because we can't "put away" bitterness without it. Remember, forgiveness is for us! We must forgive to release ourselves from prison, not our offenders. Forgiveness is the act of pardoning an offender. In Greek, it means to "let go" or as I like to say, "put away." Paul reminded us of what Jesus said in Acts 20:35, which says that it's more blessed to give than to receive. So, through the blessings and power of God, I have been able to loan money to many people. Through His same power, He has given me the ability to "let go," "put away," or "forgive" them of their debt to me to conserve the relationship because they couldn't or simply failed to repay. Forgiveness is an incredibly potent tool bestowed upon us by God, enabling us not only to uproot the seed of bitterness but to eradicate it before it takes root, marking the second stage of this debilitating ailment, which we'll discuss in detail in the next chapter. Until then, let's look at the third way, besides focusing on His love for us and cultivating forgiveness, that He has shown me how to "put away" bitterness.

The third and last effective way we are going to explore in this chapter to "put away" bitterness is by Remembering God's promises. There are so many promises we can focus on, but I just want to focus on three found in Proverbs that will be easy to remember in your time of turbulent turmoil:

1. Vengeance in the Lord's not yours:

Proverbs 20:22 ISV
Don't say, "I'll avenge that wrong!" Wait on the LORD, and he will deliver you.

2. God rewards forgiveness:

Proverbs 25:21-22 ISV
If your enemy hunger, give him food to eat; and if he thirsts, give him water to drink. For you'll be piling burning coals of shame on his head, and the LORD will reward you.

3. When we repent and forsake, we receive mercy:

Proverbs 28:13 ISV
Whoever hides his transgressions will not succeed, but whoever confesses and forsakes them will find mercy.

So, if you've been hurt and now you are bitter, try this because it's much better than festering in bitterness, which destroys and deteriorates everything it touches. Meditate on these promises to allow them to move you to "put away" bitterness because it's never worth holding on to it. The Word or Promises of God will till your hearts into fertile ground for the Holy Spirit to work. Bitterness is tough, and you will need God's help to put it away permanently. Don't ever forget that bitterness is not something you have or something you don't have; it's something you cultivate, develop, and grow.

When you get hurt, the seed of bitterness is planted. If not dealt with properly by acknowledging it, giving it to God, and forgiving the perpetrator to truly "put it away," it will be cultivated and grow roots, which is the second phase of this forbidden fruit of bitterness.

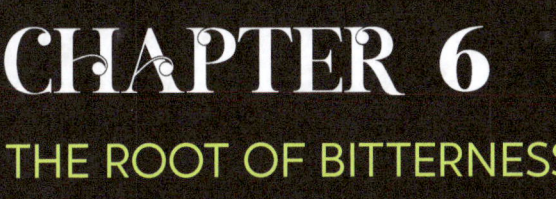

CHAPTER 6

THE ROOT OF BITTERNESS

As I am writing this book, winter is ending, and spring is starting, which means it's time to get the yard back in shape from its' dormant state. The birds and insects have come out of hibernation; the flowers and shrugs are starting to blossom and bloom into beautiful arrays of colors; the squirrels and rabbits are back to their old routine of playing and gathering for the next season; the leaves on the trees are beginning to grow back to fill the gaps to hide us from our neighbors once again; and the grass that was once in dormant is turning from brown back to green. However, every year, throughout the winter, I noticed patches of green throughout the yard. I know it's not anything I planted, but regardless of my efforts and desires, it's still there. These green patches in the midst of my brown yard are the very things I love to hate, called weeds that had been planted there somehow. Jesus tells us a parable in Matthew 13:24-30 about how the kingdom of heaven is like a farmer who sowed good seed in his field, but when he was asleep, his enemy sowed weeds among the wheat. Now, the seeds of the weeds were there all the time, but they went undetectable or unnoticeable until they started growing up with the wheat. However, when it was all said and done, the wheat was harvested, but the weeds were gathered, bound in bundles, and burned.

This reminds me of what happens when we get hurt, and the seed of bitterness is planted in our hearts, but it's undetectable because we don't know what it looks like. So, because we don't do anything to pluck up the seed of bitterness, it begins to grow roots in the moist, deep darkness of sorrow and pain until it gets strong enough to start breaking through the now shallow ground of our broken hearts to rear its ugly head of hatred, harshness, and hostility. Because we didn't deal with the seed properly, we are now faced with a bigger problem in the roots that's much harder to dig up and dispose of before it ruins the entire harvest of our lives.

Hebrews 12:15 NKJV
Look after each other so that none of you fails to receive the grace of God. Watch out that no poisonous root of bitterness grows up to trouble you, corrupting many.

Has someone hurt you, and time has passed, and the pain is growing deeper and deeper that you can't shake it off?

If this describes what is happening to you, sit down, take a deep breath, and prepare yourself to do some spring cleaning to uproot some weeds that have been growing underneath the ground in your heart all winter and are now ready to rear their ugly head.

My mom, God bless her soul, was one of the best gardeners I knew. Every spring, she would get me to help her prepare the yard, flower bed, and garden against weeds. Now, if you know anything about weeds, you can't just pull them up from the top; you must pull them up from the roots; otherwise, they are guaranteed to grow back and even fiercer than the first. Moreover, if you fail to address them effectively, they are likely to attract more and more of their weedy companions, ultimately leaving your yard in a worse state than before.

We serve a very intentional God. So, it is not an accident that God uses the image of a weed to describe this particular sin called bitterness, which has a way of creeping into all of our hearts without us detecting it until it's almost too late.

Do not be deceived; bitterness is not one of those BIG recognizable sins like anger, rebellion, or disobedience that you can see growing above the surface of our hearts through our actions. Bitterness is what I like to call a low-key or hibernating sin that grows beneath the surface where it's dark and deep, and the tears from the pain have watered the soil of our broken hearts to produce malicious actions.

Paul, who is believed to be the author of Hebrews, warns us to watch out that no poisonous root of bitterness grows to trouble us. This tells me that if we can see it, then we don't have to watch out for it. So, this poisonous root of bitters will sprout up out of nowhere one day, and when, not if, it does, it will cause trouble and corrupt many. In other words, if that poisonous bitter root is not dwelt with properly and keeps growing, there will be a massive harvest of pain for you and the people involved in your life. The toughest part about all of this is bitterness is a weed that's planted in the fertile broken soil of your heart that causes you to behave in a certain way that can't be modified by shear will-power, but you need the mighty and powerful hand of God to help kill it from the root and heal your broken heart.

I am going to step out of my comfort zone to be as vulnerable as I can to allow others to see the trauma, hurt, and pain in my life as a Pastor. I want to be very transparent about my inability to handle the hurt and pain on my own. I will honestly say that even servants of God need His help to deal with the deeply rooted matter of bitterness. No one is exempt from being hurt, let down, and disappointed by people, especially by the ones close to you. Usually, a stranger can't hurt you nearly as quickly or as much as a loved one can simply because they don't mean as much. Our expectations of those living side by side with us are so high that when they don't have your back, you fall hard; when they hit low, it really hurts and most times very hard to get over; when they clap, it's usually so loud that the ringing of what they said never stop sounding in your ears. I have seen many families destroyed because someone did or said something that no one expected and wasn't properly addressed, and therefore, the pain grew deeper to where it separated the hurt from the hurter. I have witnessed many relationships demoralized because someone said something so hurtful that they couldn't hit the delete button to erase it. Therefore, a wall was built that separated them because they couldn't get around it. I've learned a few things about these types of tests, trials, and tribulations because I've had to live through them to teach others how to do the same.

- People have talked about me behind my back, and I got wind of it, but they have no idea I know, so they pretend they love me in my face while all the time they secretly hate me. Has this happened to you?

- I have friends and family members who say they love me, but never support me, which causes their actions to speak much louder than their words. Can you relate to this?

- I have been overlooked and bypassed by leadership not because of a lack of talent, skills, or gifting, but because of fear and jealousy. Have you ever experienced this level of neglect?

This doesn't feel good, and if not handled properly, the seed of bitterness can be planted, and if not uprooted, the root of bitterness will grow deep to support all the outward fruit of misaligned behavior that's coming. So, Overcoming Life's Greatest Pains is imperative; while not easy, it's essential if you seek peace and aim to fulfill your highest potential with others and with God.

Mark 4:28 NKJV
For the earth yields crops by itself: first the blade, then the head, after that the full grain in the head.

There are three stages in the production of a harvest. We have already discussed the first stage, which is "The Seed of Bitterness" that's planted by hurt and pain, and if not acknowledged, given to God, forgiven, and put away, it will produce the second phase, which is "The Root of Bitterness."

I really believe bitterness is effective at destroying so many lives because people are unaware of it and how it is developed. Please understand that our hearts are like the soil of the earth that yields fruit automatically from the seed of words and deeds planted in it. There is a saying that we all have heard, *"Sticks and stones may break my bones, but words will never hurt me."* This is a fairytale lie from the pit of hell! We were taught this growing up and even taught it to our children because it sounds good and even soothing to a hurting person. But little did we know, it was deceptive to make us think that what others say, as well as what we say, doesn't matter. This is so far from the truth that it has enslaved and held us captive to do nothing about it so that it can grow roots to support the fruits that will be planted again and again to repeat the violent cycle of bitterness. Many of us find ourselves sounding like our parents and doing as they did, not realizing we are continuing a destructive pattern that needs to stop because it's burying our children underneath the already mounds of obstacles that they must overcome just to make it a little further than us. This generational overdose of bitterness passed down from one era to the next must stop, and it must stop now because it's killing progress. The word of God says:

Proverbs 18:20-21 NKJV
A man's stomach shall be satisfied from the fruit of his mouth; From the produce of his lips he shall be filled. Death and life are in the power of the tongue, And those who love it will eat its fruit.

This is the truth that will free us from believing the lie that words don't matter. When you speak, you have the choice to speak life or death in your life as well as the lives of others. Also, when spoken to, you can accept or deny the words of life and death spoken to you. If you don't understand this and proceed to do this, the seed of the words spoken will be planted in your heart and begin to produce roots of life or roots of death that lead to the roots of better or bitter. So, make sure you never say things like this to your children:

- *"When you grow up, you're not going to amount to nothing!"* This is a seed that can be accepted or rejected, but most likely accepted because kids don't know how to reject the words from the people they admire and look up to for direction.

- *"You are dumb and stupid, and if you don't get it together, you're going to be in a world of trouble!"* This is a seed that can be accepted or rejected, but again, it is most likely accepted and comes to pass in the lives of those who believe it.

- *"You are sorry and trifling to do anything worth doing, which is why you're not going to be anything important in life and end up in jail, alone, or dead."* This is a seed that can be accepted or rejected, but again, it is most likely accepted and comes to pass in the lives of those who believe it.

We must understand that we prophesy over our children, others, and ourselves when we open our mouths to speak. We decide to plant seeds of life or death in the hearts of those who hear that will eventually bring forth that which is spoken. This is why no one is exempt from hurt and pain. You can be the recipient and/or the issuer. One thing that I discovered is, that hurting people hurts people, which is not good because it happens automatically.

For this reason, it's important to acknowledge your bitterness and be determined to do something about it. Many of you reading this right now have been hurt and dealing with the root of bitterness because you didn't uproot the seed of bitterness caused by the hurt and pain. On the flip side, you don't realize that we usually produce after our kind. So, your actions derived from your inner inflictions have produced a lot of hurt and pain that now plants the same seeds of bitterness in others that have the potential to develop into the root of bitterness if not recognized and uprooted promptly.

Matthew 13:30 CEV
Leave the weeds alone until harvest time. Then, I'll tell my workers to gather the weeds, and tie them up, and burn them. But I'll have them store the wheat in my barn."

Again, weeds in the Bible represented something evil that was unavoidable but must be dealt with and burned in the end. Weeds in your yard are like roaches in your house; once discovered, you want to get rid of them. You will pay whatever amount of money to exterminate them because they cause more trouble than they are worth. So, I absolutely hate weeds! I don't know where they come from or why, but I wish they go back to the pit of hell from whence they came. I truly believe that, like bitterness, weeds are from the devil. If you don't pluck them up from the roots, they will grow right back. If the seed of bitterness is not dealt with or uprooted promptly, just like seeds of weeds, it will produce roots of bitterness that can't just be cut off at the top with a simple *"I'm sorry."* It must be dug up from the roots, or it will grow again after some time. So, this second section of the book is going to tackle the undetectable and elusive seed of bitterness that was never dealt with or uprooted, which is now growing down first to establish a strong foundational root of bitterness system in your heart before it makes it upward transition to produce fruit, which will be discussed later.

Again, the root of bitterness is the second phase of this deadly disease, disfunction, and disorder. This is the phase that's still underground and can't be visibly seen with the natural eye but can possibly be felt by the movement of the ground underneath through certain actions. Your heart is aching so much that it's beginning to shake things up to where you can't hide things as much as you used to. You were a master of disguise, but now everyone, including your spouse, family, and friends, is beginning to feel the sharp edges of the hidden blades of your sharp tongue, malicious deeds, and blatant disrespect. This is a very dangerous place to be because, at this very pivotal point, the heart has been affected, and as we know from the heart flow, the issues of life. If your heart has been affected by the root of bitterness, you must act now.

Note: To go more in-depth about The Root of Bitterness, please follow the link below to watch my YouTube video to learn how to uproot bitterness to prevent it from growing and destroying you and everything around you:

https://www.fhlccltd.com/videos
(Hover over Video Lessons and select "Root of Bitterness")

(Please don't forget to Like, Follow, and Subscribe to my YouTube Channel and submit prayer requests on website)

CHAPTER 7

GUARDIANS OF THE HEART: HOW TO PROTECT YOUR EMOTIONAL SANCTUARY

Writing this book is very painful because I must recall so many painful betraying acts that were done to me that broke my heart into a million pieces. I have been hurt, mistreated, used, lied to and lied against, talked about, and thoroughly betrayed by people very near and dear to me. I am not being transparent like the sun is on a sunny day to get you to shine your empathetic light on me. No, I am sharing this to help you understand that no one is exempt from the treacherous trials of life to cut so deep that it takes more than stitches to close and time to heal. These unforgettable seeds of pain and visions of betrayal are not easily erased because they are planted in our hearts. If we don't pull the plug on the continuous reel, which is replaying the unbelievable disappointment, the projector will run on repeat until our hearts are damaged and defiled. So, let's continue as we learn to guard our hearts to protect our emotional sanctuaries. Listen to what Jesus said:

Mark 7:20-23 ESV
And he said, "What comes out of a person is what defiles him. For from within, out of the heart of man, come evil thoughts, sexual immorality, theft, murder, adultery, coveting, wickedness, deceit, sensuality, envy, slander, pride, foolishness. All these evil things come from within, and they defile a person."

There is a lot of mystery in the world today as to why people do what they do, but Jesus makes it very clear and plain how human life works. Our behavior flows out of a fully functioning heart, or inner person. The word "heart" is used over seven hundred times in the Bible. The Biblical heart is not the same as the physical heart; it encompasses every aspect of our inner person. It is basically our "soul" or mind (thoughts), will (desires), and emotions (feelings) that control our actions. You usually don't do anything before you think about doing it. Our heart is our control center and must be protected at all costs. This is why King Solomon tells us:

Proverbs 4:23 NIV
Above all else, guard your heart, for everything you do flows from it.

I wish I could sell heart insurance that works like car insurance to protect our valuable means of transportation in the case of damage. We must guard and protect our hearts at all costs because what comes out of a person defiles a person.

- If you want to know why there is so much evil in the world, it's because of the condition or bitterness in the heart.

- If you want to know why there is so much sexual immorality, deceit, and confusion in the world, it's because of the condition or bitterness in the heart.

- If you want to know why there is so much pride and foolishness in the world, it's because of the condition or bitterness in the heart.

- If you want to know why there is so much sickness and disease in the world, it's because of the condition or bitterness in the heart.

3 John 1:2 NKJV
Beloved, I pray that you may prosper in all things and be in health, just as your soul prospers.

It is clearer to me now, more than ever before, that we prosper in all things, even our health, as our soul *(mind, will, and emotions)* prospers. If we have a healthy soul, full of God's Word and free of bitters, we will prosper and be in good health. If we do not have a healthy soul, because it's full of worldly ways and bitterness, we will not prosper and be in good health. The world will look just like it looks right now and even worse because our relationships are unhealthy, which makes our societies unhealthy with filth, soot, and moral decay everywhere. We must learn to forgive, not because people deserve it but because we have been forgiven by the Father. Remember, forgiveness is for you, not the other person. Forgiveness is food for the soul or heart.

It's vital to our well-being that we focus on the condition of our hearts by being the best gardener we can be by pulling up the roots of bitterness that were planted years ago by the seeds of trauma, hurt, and pain. Many people today are dealing with the roots of bitterness from their childhood bullies who tortured them. They are having problems in relationships because they can't trust their mate; they don't believe their mate; they avoid their mates because they were hurt by people who were hurting from the rejection of their past. Remember, hurting people hurts people because their hearts are too broken to mend their own to speak and do good to mend and help protect others.

James 3:11 NET
A spring does not pour out fresh water and bitter water from the same opening. Does it?

This is something that I must watch very carefully. My mother had a very sharp tongue, and my wife reminds me that I have a very sharp tongue as well. When I believe you have done something wrong to me without just cause before, I know it; I have cut you with my words. This is a reflex that I'm working on, but it comes from the overflow of my heart of things that may have happened that I never dealt with. Now, when the smallest little thing happens, it all comes spilling over, leaving devastating results like the lava of an erupting volcano. To control this, I am often reminded of the words of Jesus, which are spoken in:

Matthew 12:34 NKJV

Brood of vipers! How can you, being evil, speak good things? For out of the abundance of the heart, the mouth speaks.

When this happens, I immediately take a pulse of what's in abundance in my hurt.

- Is it hurt I didn't deal with?

- Is it pain that I pushed to the side?

- Is it disrespect I ignored?

- Is it neglect I feel that has taken place?

- Is it ingratitude that may have transpired one too many times?

Regardless of what it's from, there are no excuses to use my tongue as a defensive mechanism. Jesus just told us that our words come from our hearts, but more importantly, the words we have in abundance come from our mouths. So, whatever is coming out is an indication of what you have in abundance in your heart – good or bad. So, just as a fountain cannot produce fresh water and bitter water from the same source, likewise, our hearts cannot produce sweet and bitter words at the same time. Those who are bitter with their words don't have a right heart at that moment. Our words are a huge indicator of what's in our hearts. Therefore, we must pull up the roots of bitterness from our lives because not only is it hurting us, but it will turn around and hurt others at the same time.

So, to overcome this root of bitterness, not only must we protect our hearts to control what comes out to defile or corrupt us and others, but we must understand to do this, we must be willing and desire to be peacemakers. So, ask yourself, "Am I bitter, or do I have a desire to live in peace with others?

CHAPTER 8

EMBRACING SERENITY: THE PATHWAY TO LIVING IN PEACE AMIDST CHAOS

"Peace is not something you wish for; it is something you make, something you are, something you do, and something you give away."
Robert Fulghum

When I think about someone who exemplifies this, my wife comes to mind because she is the very epitome of peace in our relationship. Every relationship needs someone who understands the vitality of peace. If things get heated, she knows exactly when to shut it down and what not to say to keep the peace. That's not to say we will not gain closure in the situation; she will bring it back up when heated waters are simmered down to a peaceable level to continue boiling out the impurities. Matthew tells us in chapter 5 and verse 9 that blessed are the peacemakers, and God knows our relationship is blessed because we both have learned the pathway to living in peace with one another, which doesn't mean accepting any and everything but dealing with it in a sensible and godly manner.

Hebrews 12:14 NLT
Work at living in peace with everyone, and work at living a holy life, for those who are not holy will not see the Lord.

It's time for us to take a new grip on life despite the pain that planted the seed of bitterness, and because it wasn't addressed, it has now turned into the root of bitterness, which is harder, but not impossible to uproot with the help of the Master Planter, God. We need God's help to heal our broken hearts because a lame or hurting person cannot navigate the same environment as a healed and whole person. So, just like Christ is our example, we must allow His light to shine through us where it conducts our lives in a way that those who are weak (substance abuse, physical abuse, sexual abuse, mental abuse, religious abuse) due to bitterness can follow our example and be healed, delivered and set free from their pain that has developed into a root of bitterness that has them bound.

As Christians, it is our duty and calling to live in peace with everyone. Jesus preached in the Beatitudes in Matthew 5:9, *"Blessed are the peacemakers, for they will be called children of God."* I don't know about you, but nothing supersedes my desire to be a child of God. According to scripture:

- Making peace with those who hurt us is a way to be called a child of God.

- Making peace by forgiving those who despitefully use us is a way to be called a child of God.

- Making peace by loving those who hate us is another way to be called a child of God.

- Making peace by putting away bitterness is a way to be called a child of God.

Peace must be at the forefront of our agenda because Scripture instructs us to walk in a peaceful, loving, and meek manner that will not cause others to stumble and fall into bitterness. Please understand that being meek is not being weak, as many believe. Being meek is having power without power having you. Jesus was the meekest person to ever walk the earth. Being meek is simply power under control. In other words, you have the power to be mad, angry, and upset to hurt those who hurt you, but instead, you choose not to for the sake of keeping the peace, which displays your meekness that will eventually lead you into the blessings of God.

Thus, if we don't allow the poison, sour, brackish taste of bitterness to cause us to walk in sin, God can use us to walk in a holy manner so that others will see Him in and through our lives. Knowing that you are living right and treating others right brings forth a sense of peace that's priceless. Peace that surpasses all understanding can only come from God. If we trust God and keep our minds focused on Him, He will keep us in perfect peace (Isaiah 26:3). God is the only One that heals the pains from our past and gives us the strength to pull up the root of bitterness that has grown so deep that it's dictating our behavior.

Philippians 4:4-7 NKJV
Rejoice in the Lord always. Again, I will say, rejoice! Let your gentleness be known to all men. The Lord is at hand. Be anxious for nothing, but in everything by prayer and supplication, with thanksgiving, let your requests be made known to God; and the peace of God, which surpasses all understanding, will guard your hearts and minds through Christ Jesus.

Paul just told us that peace is the secret ingredient to guarding our hearts and minds through Christ Jesus. Here are the secrets to gaining God's peace amid your heartache and pain.

1. We must learn to rejoice in the Lord always, even when someone hurts us, because now, we know who they are and what they are capable of doing.
2. We must learn to be gentle to them and how we handle their sinful act toward us to keep the bitterness from setting in to destroy us while they walk free.
3. We must learn, no matter how we are feeling, not to be anxious, which is another word for pride because we are so focused on how we feel, what they did to us, and what we are going to do about it instead of what God promised to do about it.
4. We must learn to pray, humble ourselves, and ask God to heal and strengthen us to exemplify Him and His love through it all.
5. We must learn to thank God for hearing us, healing us, and helping us not to be easily offended to allow the root of bitterness to come.

I tell you, when we have carefully done these five biblical steps, as promised, the peace of God, which surpasses all understanding, will guard your hearts and minds through Christ Jesus.

Romans 12:18 NKJV
If it is possible, as much as depends on you, live peaceably with all men.

We must do everything thing we possibly can to live in peace with one another. I don't care how much you have been hurt; we must lean on God to help us live in peace with the very people who hurt us. If Jesus did it and He told us to be imitators of Him, then we can do it as well. Now, I am going to tell you something that may sound a little unorthodox, but if you follow me, it will sound better as you digest it through your understanding.

It has been said that the best way to avoid catching a cold is not to be around a person with a cold. If the cold virus doesn't enter your body, you can't contract a cold. Likewise, one of the best ways to not get infected with the disease of bitterness is not to allow the seed of bitterness to be planted in you. One of the best ways to do this is by not putting unrealistic expectations on others. Many times, bitterness comes when someone hurts or disappoints us because we expected them to do something, and they did not do it, or we didn't expect them to do something that they did. If you don't expect anything from others, they can't let you down, but if they do something good that you didn't expect, it will bring forth great joy. I know this sounds a little harsh and very unrealistic, and many will not agree with it, but I challenge you to try it before you dismiss it.

Jeremiah 17:9 NKJV
"The heart is deceitful above all things, And desperately wicked; Who can know it?

Believe it or not, you don't even know your own heart. Your heart can deceive you if you are not careful because, at its very root, it's wicked. Some people know exactly what they are doing, but I don't believe most people want to deliberately hurt other people. Not to give anyone an excuse, because there are none. But because our hearts are naturally wicked and people do not always know this, things just happen. They may say one thing and do another, not because they want to, but because something happens within. Their initial intentions were to do exactly what they said, but time, thoughts, and temptations happen between what they said and what they did. Several Hebrew meanings for heart can help explain how this can happen. The Hebrew word for heart here means feelings, will, intellect, understanding, and mind. So, when we get in our feelings, our minds begin to play tricks on us to shape our wills, intellect, and understanding to do things we know we shouldn't be doing. This is why we should not operate out of the realm of our feelings, and one major reason is that the enemy of our souls resides there through his power of suggestions.

Consequently, if we are not mindful of this, we will always hurt, disappoint, and frustrate people, whether we desire to or not. So, we can bless ourselves by throwing away expectations, especially unrealistic expectations that we put on others, which is not fair anyway because they will most likely not fulfill them. Many relationships fail due to unrealistic expectations that are never met. The only person we should put expectations on is our Lord, who will never leave us, nor forsake us because He loves us, His heart is pure and can't change and will remain the same yesterday, today, and forevermore (Hebrews 13:5-8). We can always trust in Him, His Word, His Works, and His Timing, because He's always on time and never late. Releasing our expectations of others and putting it on Him to receive His perfect way exposes our trust in Him, which ultimately benefits us no matter how we look at it.

Now, I know this warrants more explanation, but I am asking you to trust me because it would take me a long time to go in-depth on this subject. This subject is so deep that I can write an entire book on it. However, if you want more content on expectations, especially unrealistic expectations, and how detrimental they can be to your relationships, let me direct you to my other book, "If Only I Knew Before I Said I Do." I go into further detail on how to avoid this trap that will enslave you and ruin your relationships.

2 Thessalonians 3:16 NKJV
Now may the Lord of peace Himself give you peace always in every way. The Lord be with you all.

Now, none of this is the easiest to do, and why we need the grace of God to do it. When the grace of God is upon us, He gives us the ability to do what we can't do in our strength.

So, we will not only be able to protect our hearts to live in peace, but our desires will become His desires also, and we know He desires for us to love and be there for one another, just like He is there for us all. So, the question you need to ask yourself is, "Are you there for your fellow brothers and sisters?" If you need help honestly answering this very important question, continue reading to pull back the layers of your freedom.

CHAPTER 9

UNITED IN CARE: NURTURING EACH OTHER'S WELL-BEING

Hebrews 12:15 NKJV
Look after each other so that none of you fails to receive the grace of God. Watch out that no poisonous root of bitterness grows up to trouble you, corrupting many.

No one I know wants to fail God or fail to receive the grace of God. God's grace consists of God giving us what we don't deserve, which is different from God's mercy, which is God not giving what we do deserve. God's grace is a gift and can't be earned, which means contrary to popular belief, our actions do not earn the grace of God. If it did, that wouldn't be considered grace.

Romans 11:6 NKJV
And if by grace, then it is no longer of works; otherwise, grace is no longer grace. But if it is of works, it is no longer grace; otherwise, work is no longer work.

Therefore, we don't fall from grace by not being holy enough to earn it. Paul often speaks of falling from grace by putting faith in our works instead of having our faith firmly placed in Christ and what He did for us.

Galatians 5:4 NKJV
You have become estranged from Christ, you who attempt to be justified by law; you have fallen from grace.

I know many people who try to get rid of this deadening root of bitterness on their own. They fall prey to its alluring temptations of pride to do it themselves to only remain entangled more in the stringy roots that continue to grow down before they go up; hence, why we must look to Christ, who is grace to give us what we don't deserve in order to look out for each other so that we don't, and they don't fail to receive grace to Overcome Life's Greatest Pains that caused the root of bitterness to remain.

At the end of the day, bitterness is a bad, acidic poison that's like a sour, brackish taste in our mouths that contaminates our hearts with strong animosity, resentfulness, and disappointment that doesn't just hurt or poison us but those around us as well. Again, we are supposed to walk in a manner that positively influences others. If we get bitter, that bitterness will spread and affect others just like cancer spreads and affects other organs in the body. This is one reason Hebrews 12:15 tells us to look after each other so that no one fails to receive the grace of God. If we don't watch out for this poisonous root of bitterness, it will grow up to trouble us as well as defile and corrupt many. So, this second phase, the root of bitterness, is like the second phase or stage of cancer, which, if caught in time, you can be saved from its deadly nature to spread and destroy everything in its path.

We must look out for each other and not let bitterness blow out the candle of our peace, happiness, and joy to leave our souls in bitter darkness. People do what people do; sinners do what sinners do; and bitter sinful people do what bitter sinful people do – they do hurtful things. If someone tells you who they are by hurting you, believe them, forgive them, walk in peace with them, and look out for them to receive grace from God to protect your heart and put all bitterness away so that it will not take root to trouble you and defile or corrupt others. Look at the life of Jesus and how He allows His light to forever shine in darkness to show us the way:

- Jesus was lied against, but He didn't retaliate.

- Jesus was slapped, and He turned the other cheek.

- Jesus was mocked and didn't say a mumbling word.

- Jesus was beaten and didn't resist so that we could be healed.

- Jesus was pierced to be able to wipe away our tears.

- Jesus was hung high and stretched wide in crucifixion, where He bled for the forgiveness of our past, present, and future sins.

- Jesus died on that old rugged cross to ensure we didn't have to.

- Jesus was buried in that borrowed tomb as a sacrifice of life for us to live.

- Jesus went to hell to conquer Satan and his fallen angels to make us more than conquerors.

- Jesus rose with all power so that we can do as He did to win by not allowing the root of bitterness to set in.

- Jesus is now seated at the right hand of the Father, praying and making intercession for us to be victorious over the enemy and everything he brings, including bitterness to defeat us.

Jesus looked out for us so that we would receive the Holy Spirit to give us the strength and anointing to look out for one another. If I genuinely look out for you, I'm going to make sure no hurt, harm, or danger is going to come near you, especially from me. We need to treat others in the way we want to be treated, which is one of the greatest ways we can look out for one another.

Matthew 7:12 NKJV
Therefore, whatever you want men to do to you, do also to them, for this is the Law and the Prophets.

This is considered the Golden Rule, which is to treat others in the way that you would like to be treated. To take it a step further, it falls into the second greatest command Jesus gave us, which is to love our fellow brothers and sisters as we love ourselves.

Matthew 22:36-40 NKJV
"Teacher, which is the great commandment in the law?" Jesus said to him, 'YOU SHALL LOVE THE LORD YOUR GOD WITH ALL YOUR HEART, WITH ALL YOUR SOUL, AND WITH ALL YOUR MIND.' This is **the** *first and great commandment. And* **the** *second* **is** *like it: 'YOU SHALL LOVE YOUR NEIGHBOR AS YOURSELF.' On these two commandments hang all the Law and the Prophets."*

If we love God, we will love His people; if we love God, we will treat His people like we want to be treated; if we love God, we will look out for each other. We are living in a world with so many unnecessary and solvable problems. God has given us solutions for everything, but we must be willing to drop our pride, realize we don't know everything, humble ourselves, and follow His ways instead of ours. Think about it: if we just looked out for each other or treated others the way we wanted to be treated, there would really be no need for any of the laws that govern our actions.

- I wouldn't cheat you because I wouldn't want you to cheat me.

- I wouldn't be unfaithful to you because I wouldn't want you to be unfaithful to me.

- I wouldn't murder you because I wouldn't want you to murder me.

- I wouldn't deceive you because I wouldn't want you to deceive me.

- I wouldn't lie on or to you because I wouldn't want you to lie on or to me.

- I wouldn't steal from you because I wouldn't want you to steal from me.

I believe you got the picture. Truthfully, loving God and loving others as we love ourselves would solve many, if not all, the social problems of today. This would stop the massive spread or epidemic of bitterness that's destroying our world. Loving God and embracing what He loves—His people—acts as the vaccine against the contagious viral disease of bitterness, which is seeded within us by pain and hurt. Because it was not uprooted, it developed roots. If left untreated, it will bear fruit that is harmful for anyone to consume. Jesus Overcame Life's Greatest Pains, and now we have access to His grace to do the same. However, if we fail to care for one another, the pain will persist in sowing seeds; nurturing these seeds by reliving the hurt will allow roots to develop. If these roots are not uprooted, they will yield fruit that is poisonous to all who partake.

CHAPTER 10

THE FORBIDDEN FRUIT OF BITTERNESS

In the beginning, God created man, Adam, from the dust of the ground and breathed into him the breath of life to become a living being created in their image and likeness. From that very same ground, God made every tree pleasant to our sight as well as to our tongue from the fruit that it bared. Now, there were two special trees in the midst of the garden, the tree of life and the tree of knowledge of good and evil, which came with very specific life and death instructions from God. He told Adam that he could freely eat from every tree in the garden except the tree of knowledge of good and evil because he would surely die if he did. Shortly after, God recognized that it wasn't good for man to be alone, so He made woman from man, and they became one. All was good in the land of paradise until Lucifer, the fallen angel, was hurt because he was kicked out of heaven due to his pride and rebellion, which planted the seed of bitterness in him to now destroy everything good that God had made. So, he bypasses Adam, who had direct instructions from God, and attacks Eve, who had secondhand instructions from Adam, where he questions the truth that she thought she knew when he said, *"Has God indeed said, 'You shall not eat of every tree of the garden'?"* Eve made the biggest mistake we all make when we respond to his nonsense. Anyway, you know how the story goes from here. Because she entertained his suggestions, which is one of his weapons, she was deceived and distracted from focusing on all that God had given them to the one thing He didn't. The same thing happens to us when we focus on what we don't have instead of being grateful for all we have. So, she ate the forbidden fruit and gave it to her husband, who was with her, and he ate, and their eyes were opened, and spiritual as well as physical death entered the earth. If Adam had effectively communicated with Eve and obeyed God, regardless of what she did, we would not be in the mess we are in today. However, because He didn't and fell prey to pride, rebellion, disobedience, and peer pressure, he ate the forbidden fruit; sin entered the world and brought the bitter effects of death with it, which ushered in our need for a Savior in Jesus to conquer sin and death with His life so that we wouldn't have to live with the bitterness that came from disobediently partaking of the forbidden fruit (Genesis 1-3). The forbidden fruit ruined relationships then, and it is still ruining relationships today. I thank God that He didn't allow Adams's disobedience to hurt Him and plant the seed of bitterness Him to produce the fruit of bitterness found in His wrath. Instead, His love, gracious and merciful nature kicked in to forgive, protect, and provide a better way through Jesus and His obedience to reconcile mankind's relationship with God by destroying sin to make all who are willing righteous (Romans 5:19).

Ephesians 4:31-32 NET
You must put away all bitterness, anger, wrath, quarreling,
and slanderous talk – indeed all malice. Instead, be kind to
one another, compassionate, forgiving one another, just as
God in Christ also forgave you.

Did someone plant the seed of pain in you, but instead of addressing it to diffuse it, you didn't do anything to resolve it?

Has that pain developed roots that have extended to other areas of your life to where you can no longer hide how you feel?

Are fruits of bitterness that started as a seed that once lay dormant or unnoticeable on the inside now manifesting on the outside as fruits of anger and rage toward your betrayer and even others?

If this is a depiction of you and how you feel, you need help before that very thing destroys you and everything around you. Just like Jesus was the answer from the beginning, He is still the answer to neutralizing the effects of bitterness that was ingested from eating the forbidden fruit caused by the pain, hurt, disappointment, and trauma.

The Lord has helped me Overcome Life's Greatest Pains, which have deposited bitterness in me. I attempted to address it on my own, but instead found myself plunging deeper and deeper into its unfathomable depths. It would appear in the form of depression, anger, cynicism, and even abandonment. It was solely through the power of God and the wisdom from His Word that I was healed and empowered to resist the enemy's temptations of revenge and overcome his trap of incessantly replaying the painful acts of betrayal, deceit, disappointment, and lack of support. The devil's mission is to steal, kill, and destroy us because that's all he knows how to do. He knows if he can get us to live in our pain, he can get us to die in our pain. Consequently, we will never achieve our purpose, never reach our destiny, and never be able to defeat him and his army by helping save others from this awful entrapment.

As we have learned, pain plants the seed of bitterness that, if not resolved, will naturally start to produce the roots of bitterness that grow deeper and deeper until they are strong enough to support the fruit of bitterness. The seed and root of bitterness are all on the inside and not visible to others, but very detrimental to you. You are mad all the time: everything gets on your nerves; you don't want to be around people; you don't believe anything anyone says; you feel like everyone is out to get you, which are all inner feelings unseen by others because you have become good at hiding or faking the funk. If not rectified, these feelings that were once on the inside get stronger and stronger until one day, the fruit breaks through into the outside in the shape of your actions of rebellion, dis-respect, argumentation, disobedience, confrontational, and malice. What was once in the dark or hidden is now in the light and seen as well as felt by others. Listen to what Jesus said in:

Luke 12:2 NKJV
For there is nothing covered that will not be revealed, nor hidden that will not be known.

Now, as we have discovered, there are three stages in the production of a harvest. We have already discussed the first stage, which is **"The Seed of Bitterness,"** that is planted by pain. If not acknowledged, forgiven, given to God, and put away, it will produce the second stage, which is **"The Root of Bitterness,"** if not taken care of, darkness will enter our hearts to chase away all peace. Time of unresolved issues passes until it strengthens to harvest the third stage, which is the most destructive stage called **"The Forbidden Fruit of Bitterness."**

Again, bitterness is poisonous and toxic. When we choose bitterness over forgiveness, we inflict greater pain on ourselves than on the person who hurt us. Please understand it's not the one who wounded you that is affected; it's you. As the old saying goes, refusing to forgive is like drinking poison and expecting the other person to die. Studies have shown that a rattlesnake if cornered, will sometimes become so angry that it will bite itself. When bitterness takes root, it produces the fruit of anger, wrath, hate, resentment, and malice against others, which is like biting ourselves with venomous poison. We think we are harming others when we are mad at them, but half the time, they don't even know or care that we feel a certain way. Never allow people who didn't give you joy to take it away. Never empower anyone to dictate and determine how you feel. This is way too much power to give to another human being that's not deserving.

Many people don't know, but bitterness destroys our spiritual health, mental health, physical health, and even our interpersonal relationships. God is all about developing relationships, not ruining relationships. When Adam rebelled and disobeyed to let sin in, which separated us from God, He sent Jesus to earth to reestablish His relationship with mankind because the relationship, not religion, is just that important to Him.

1 John 4:20 ESV
If anyone says, "I love God," and hates his brother, he is a liar; for he who does not love his brother whom he has seen cannot love God whom he has not seen.

It doesn't take a Prophet to discern if someone loves God; all we must do is look at how they treat or love God's people. If someone says they love God but doesn't love the people whom God created and loves, they are liars, and the truth is not in them. I love everyone, but I hate the sin that's apparent in their lives, just as God does. Relationships with the Lord will manifest love for His people regardless of their downfalls. This is one of the greatest indications of our relationship with the Lord. So, one of the key reasons why it's crucial to truly learn how to Overcome Life's Greatest Pains, which lead to bitterness, is for the reconciliation of relationships.

Note: To go more in-depth about The Fruit of Bitterness, please follow the link below to watch my YouTube video to learn how to avoid consuming the forbidden fruit of bitterness:

https://www.fhlccltd.com/videos
(Hover over Video Lessons and select "Fruit of Bitterness")

(Please don't forget to Like, Follow, and Subscribe to my YouTube Channel and submit prayer requests on website)

CHAPTER 11

BEYOND BONDS: NAVIGATING THE DEPTHS OF RELATIONSHIPS

Galatians 5:22-23 NKJV
But the fruit of the Spirit is love, joy, peace, longsuffering,
kindness, goodness, faithfulness, gentleness, self-control.
Against such, there is no law.

There are only two ways we can walk – after the spirit or after the flesh. There are only two types of fruit we are going to produce - good fruit or bad fruit- which will determine the nature of and how we navigate through our relationships. Walking after the Spirit will produce good fruit to develop good relationships, but walking after the Flesh will produce bad fruit to destroy relationships. When bitterness takes root, it produces fruit that will wound and poison anyone who tastes it.

During the summer, when the weather is hot, the sun is shining, people are out, and so are the insects. For some reason,

I find myself fighting ants every summer, no matter how many times I defeat them or think I defeat them. I have tried everything, but the only thing that seems to work well for me is a substance that looks like sand. It's actually little grains of bitter poisonous pellets that are activated by water that attract the ants. They come and eat it, but the ingenious thing about this poison is that they don't die immediately. It deceives them to think it's good for food. So, they get a mouth full and take it back to their Queen, who eats and eats and keeps eating. After some time, the bitter, poisonous pallets expand and explode in their stomachs, ultimately destroying the ant that carried it and the Queen that received it from them. So, not only was the infected ant destroyed, but also the other ants it encountered until the entire mound of ants was destroyed.

Like the ant, when we ingest bitterness, it produces the fruit of bitterness, and everyone we encounter can be infected with bitterness through our negative actions and deeds. This is why we must be led by the fruit of the Spirit (love, joy, peace, patience, kindness, goodness, faithfulness, gentleness, and self-control) so that we are not led by the fruit of bitterness (hate, sadness, wrath, impatience, rudeness, anger, quarreling, slanderous talk, and malice), in which the condition of our hearts determines both. The fruits we are supposed to produce come from our abiding relationship with Jesus. The harvest of good fruit is produced in an unhindered fellowship with Him, which then is reproduced in others. It is the process that Jesus formed when He walked the earth spreading love and preaching the Gospel that produced what we call today The Church.

For the last 2,000-plus years, we have seen a naturally re-producing, organic process formed from the few people who became Jesus' disciples in its first year of formation. Then they taught others what He had taught them, and the rest is History. Jesus said in:

John 15:13-15 NKJV
Greater love has no one than this than to lay down one's life for his friends. You are My friends if you do whatever I command you. No longer do I call you servants, for a servant does not know what his master is doing; but I have called you friends, for all things that I heard from My Father I have made known to you.

Think about this for one second to really understand how important a relationship is to our Father. Mankind crucified God's Son, Jesus, and He was still willing to lay down His life to reconcile the relationship. God looks past all the hurt and pain we still cause Him today to have a relationship with us. He has every right to be bitter because of our pride, hate, disobedience, rebellion, and rejection, but he doesn't because the relationship is more important than anything else. We should always strive to walk in God's kind of love that is characterized by putting others ahead of self (Philippians 2:3). According to Jesus, the greatest expression of self-sacrifice for others is laying down one's life. Still, it must be done from the proper motive of love.

I remember counseling a couple where their relationship was riddled with deceit and infidelity. The husband was so unfaithful that he was getting caught cheating with women and even having children outside the marriage. The wife loved him so much that she forgave him, but the hurt from the disloyalty was planted in her broken heart until it produced the fruit of bitterness. She stayed with him, but she didn't trust him, she didn't respect him, and she didn't honor him at all. So, her bitter actions hurt him, which planted the seed of bitterness in him. Now, I am facing two people who "love" one another, and want to stay with one another, but were hurting and didn't know what to do to alleviate the pain. They had every right to divorce, but they loved God and each other enough to where they wanted to honor their wedding vows:

- To have and to hold forever,
    - For better or for worse,
        - For richer or poorer,
            - In sickness and in health,
                - To love and to cherish, until death.

So, the only thing I knew to do that would work in this desperate and dire situation was to teach them about the God kind of love that never fails. To make a long story short, they are still married with children of their own, bitter-free, happy, and in love with one another again. Glory be to God!

They laid down their lives for one another, just like Jesus laid down His life for us, His friends. We are called to follow Jesus' example and go all the way to lay down our lives for one another for the sake of our relationship, which is the greatest expression of love.

Here, Jesus said we are His friends because He laid down His life for us. What an honor to be called the friend of God.

Abraham, Moses, and Enoch were just a few of those who had been called the friends of God before this time. Now, because of Jesus, we believers have been reconciled and are in a relationship with Him. Please understand that keeping the Lord's commands doesn't warrant our relationship, but if we are in a relationship with Him, we will keep His commandments.

If we do as Jesus is teaching us, by walking in the fruit of the Spirit to love one another, we are considered His friend. As He developed His relationship with us through grave sacrifice, we should do the same with others. Each one reaches one to teach one, which should be our motto! That's precisely why I don't fixate on numbers, as it only takes one transformed individual to change the world. If we overcome bitterness with love to develop long-lasting relationships, we can change this world for Jesus.

Will people still hurt you? Yes!

Will people still be wrong with you? Yes!

Will people still use you? Yes!

Understand the fact that sinner's sin and hurting people hurt people. This is what they do, and to help us from getting hurt, we shouldn't expect them to do anything other than what they have shown they are capable of doing. At the same time, if we remain focused on the relationship and not retaliation, the fruit of bitterness will not get watered to grow and separate us from one another. In order to do this and Overcome Life's Greatest Pains that lead to bitterness, we must follow the example of Jesus to develop the spirit of reconciliation, which brought us back together with the Father.

CHAPTER 12

HEALING RIFTS: THE JOURNEY TOWARDS RECONCILIATION

2 Corinthians 5:18-19 NKJV
Now all things are of God, who has reconciled us to Himself through Jesus Christ, and has given us the ministry of reconciliation, that is, that God was in Christ reconciling the world to Himself, not imputing their trespasses to them, and has committed to us the word of reconciliation.

P lease notice that four forms of reconciliation were used in this verse of scripture, which means we should pay extremely close attention to it because it's necessary. Reconcile in Greek means to change mutually by compounding differences. Reconciliation means exchanging, adjusting restoration to favor, atonement, reestablishing a close relationship between, settling, or resolving. So, to simplify it, reconciling means restoring relationships, like Jesus restored or reconciled our relationship with the Father through the atonement or payment of our sins with His perfect and sinless life. The key to reconciliation is effectively dealing with the root cause of the animosity, dislike, ill will, hatred, or hostility that has caused a dispute and separation between people. For an instant, the enmity or hostility between mankind and God was a sin. I thank God and will be eternally grateful to God because He loved us so much that He willingly gave us His Only begotten Son, Jesus, to remove the sin barrier that reconciled mankind and God as friends once again.

John 15:13-17 NKJV

Greater love has no one than this, than to lay down one's life for his friends. You are My friends if you do whatever I command you. No longer do I call you servants, for a servant does not know what his master is doing; but I have called you friends, for all things that I heard from My Father I have made known to you. You did not choose Me, but I chose you and appointed you that you should go and bear fruit, and that your fruit should remain, that whatever you ask the Father in My name He may give you. These things I command you, that you love one another.

God chose us to be His friend, and we can be His friend if we follow His commandments to love Him and love one another. It takes love to reconcile! God did all the reconciling, and man is the one who is reconciled. He didn't do it because we were deserving; God knows we were not, He did it because He loves us. Love reconciles, and when we understand this, we will be quick, not slow, to reconcile with one another by any means necessary.

Reconciliation is not just something we do; it's our ministry or service to God. This is what we do! Christians are supposed to be in the ministry of reconciling people to God. Unfortunately, we miss the mark on this from the church to the world. I've been in too many churches, heard too many sermons, and encountered too many "Christians" who are alienating people from God instead of showing them the love of God to reconcile them to Him. Now, please don't misunderstand me. We indeed need to show people their need for God to get them to receive His forgiveness and reconciliation, but the attitudes, pride, malice, anger, and bitterness with which many confront sinners are not correct. There are so many separations in relationships between husbands and wives, parents and children, siblings, friends and relatives that could be avoided if this is understood and we minister reconciliation instead of retaliation.

God was in Christ, reconciling the world to Himself. He didn't have to, but because He is love, He was compelled to do it. He couldn't have reconciled us to Himself by imputing or charging our sins against us, just like we can't reconcile with our brothers and sisters by imputing or charging their sins or acts of evil toward us to them. This is effective Christian ministering of reconciliation. Minor on the sin and major on love and grace to master reconciliation.

Romans 5:20 NKJV
Moreover, the law entered that the offense might abound. But where sin abounded, grace abounded much more,

The Word of God teaches us that we should not be easily offended because I believe when we are, we open ourselves up to bitterness. John got offended when Jesus didn't come to see him in prison, and bitterness began to set in based on his response, and things didn't turn out so well for him. Please know that bitterness is not good for you, no matter how you view it and how good it makes you feel at the moment. It is deceivingly evil because you think you are hurting someone when you are just hurting yourself. Just like poison is destructive to the body, bitterness is destructive and toxic to your soul *(mind, will, and emotions)* and body. This is one reason Scripture tells us that the root of bitterness defiles us (Hebrews 12:15). When the fruit of bitterness is produced in our lives, it brings darkness and distortion to our countenances. Our "guards stay up," so reconciliation is next to impossible. We aren't too inclined to reconcile with others like Christ reconciled us to the Father.

Isaiah 38:15 NKJV
"What shall I say? He has both spoken to me, And He Himself has done it. I shall walk carefully all my years In the bitterness of my soul.

One of Jesus' main ministries and messages was reconciliation or forgiveness because the reproduction of bad fruit will also occur if we have a wrong relationship with Christ, and unforgiveness will do this. We must forgive if we want to be forgiven (Matthew 6:14-15). It's impossible to reconcile with someone you don't forgive. Forgiveness is mandatory to bear the fruit of the Spirit; otherwise, unforgiveness will bear the fruit of bitterness. This fruit ranges from anger to outrage, from self-pity to self-centeredness, from hate to wrath, from resentment to grudges, from rebellion to defiance, from animosity to malice, and many other kinds of expressions of the fruit of bitterness. If you see these things in your life or the lives of others, you are most likely bearing the fruit of bitterness, which is not good, and relationship reconciliation is next to impossible.

Proverbs 19:11 ESV
Good sense makes one slow to anger, and it is his glory to overlook an offense.

I always like to balance things out. This scripture is very profound in informing us that a smart person or a person with good sense won't get angry quickly and will recognize that it is powerful, honorable, brave, and excellent not to be easily offended and to look past people's transgressions to forgive them. I would see couples trying to do this all the time, which is fine, but what often occurs is that they never confront the wrong and, therefore, never resolve recurring issues. Again, that which we don't confront, we can't change. If you have a flat tire and you don't confront it by changing it, you can't move forward. If you do, it will cause more damage and cost more money to repair than if you would have just confronted the issue by fixing the flat tire instead of ignoring it. The goal is to learn to confront without offending to progress. Don't allow every little thing to anger you, even though those little things can become big. However, please notice this verse never says a smart person never gets angry. We can get anger and sin, not according to the scripture found in Ephesians 4:26. I used to think that as a Christian, I couldn't get mad and upset, but I was wrong. A godly anger is part of holiness and unity. We must hate evil and disunity. If we can tolerate something, we will. Develop your intolerance for evil and disunity and learn how to reconcile to bring things back together.

Ephesians 4:26-27 NKJV
"BE ANGRY, AND DO NOT SIN": do not let the sun go down on your wrath, nor give place to the devil.

We can be angry, but it must be righteous anger that is not sin. Think about it: Jesus got angry without sinning, and if we are supposed to imitate Him, we should do the same (Mark 3:5). There is a good type of anger that is not directed at people but at evil. We need this righteous type of anger, especially in the world we live in today. We can't afford ever to let it take a rest or let the sun go down on our righteous anger.

The world is in the morally decaying state it's in now because Christians have become too passive. Our passiveness gives place to the devil, which we shouldn't do because he's already a bully. Consequently, being passive instead of angry at the devil gives place to him. We are called to resist or actively combat the devil, and this righteous indignation is a crucial aspect of a vigorous and violet mindset. So, if you are a person who struggles with anger issues, you may be able to use it as a gift by focusing on things that God hates that are evil because we are commanded to hate evil.

Romans 12:9 CEV
Be sincere in your love for others. Hate everything evil and hold tight to everything that is good.

As mentioned earlier, we are supposed to love God's people but hate the sin as He does. He has commanded us to hate evil and stay focused on everything that's good. Ephesians 6:12 basically tells us that we are not supposed to hate people because they are not our enemies. However, we are supposed to fight against evil forces, authorities, rulers of darkness, and powers in the spiritual world. So, anytime something comes against your desire to reconcile, it is most like the enemy of souls, and we must fight against that urge and reconcile.

Now again, we must have balance because there are times when hating evil will put us at odds with people. As a Pastor, I am called to speak the truth in love, and because of that, I lose people and make them mad at me because they don't want to know or hear the truth that will make them free. The truth usually hurts before it helps. So, God revealed to me that I must give people time to accept the truth, and once they get over the initial hurt, they will come back around. Nonetheless, if they don't, I've done my job. This was ground-breaking and freeing because it previously troubled me, but I grew to be okay with it because I would rather please God than man.

Proverbs 16:7 NKJV
When a man's ways please the LORD, He makes even his enemies to be at peace with him.

We are not called to like everything people do; we're only to live peaceably with everyone as much as we can, according to Romans 12:18. Sometimes, reconciliation isn't possible, and that's okay if you try. Think about it: even Jesus got angry and drove the people who were selling their cattle, sheep, doves, and the money changers from the temple with a whip because they did evil by turning the house of worship into a market-place (John 2:14-16). He got angry at evil, but not bitter. These were probably some of the same people who wanted Him crucified, but He died to reconcile them to the Father anyway. They probably rejected Him and denied His offering of recon-ciliation, which landed them in hell. He did all He could, but they had the last decision to accept Him or reject Him. Those who accept Him are reconciled to the Father, their sins are atoned for, and they receive eternal life. But those who reject Him are not reconciled to the Father, their sins are not paid for, and they receive eternal damnation. God has done all He can to reconcile us to Himself, and now we must do the rest by choosing His Son, Jesus, and making Him our Lord and Savior. Again, the choice of eternal life or eternal damnation is always ours and never God's. So, make the right choice in Him and the ministry of reconciliation to change our hearts and other's hearts, which leads me to an astronomical im-portant point discussed in the next chapter.

CHAPTER 13

FROM WITHIN: CULTIVATING THE RIGHT HEART FOR LASTING HARMONY

Psalms 51:10 NKJV
Create in me a clean heart, O God, And renew a steadfast
spirit within me.

If we truly want to Overcome Life's Greatest Pains that can lead to bitterness, like Jesus did, through remaining focused on relationship instead of retaliation; and reconciliation instead of separation, we must work on getting our hearts right through God. I know your hearts have been broken so badly that you don't even believe it can be mended to reconcile relationships through forgiving those who hurt you. Well, the good news is that the Lord created in us clean hearts and put new spirits within us for salvation. So, you can be whole again, forgive again, and cultivate the right heart within you again to live in lasting harmony with yourself and others.

When someone tries to dig up the root of bitterness in their life, their heart or the soil of their heart must be improved. This is where the nutrition of God's Word and obedience to His instructions attack the root of bitterness to kill the fruit of bitterness. We begin to see bitterness as an enemy, just as Jesus does. Bitterness is our enemy from our enemy to divide us because he knows a house divided against itself cannot stand. Listen to what Jesus said in:

Mark 3:24-26 NKJV
If a kingdom is divided against itself, that kingdom cannot stand. And if a house is divided against itself, that house cannot stand. And if Satan has risen up against himself, and is divided, he cannot stand, but has an end.

There is nothing good that can come from bitterness. It may feel good to hold on to something, but you are not the one holding on to it; it is holding on to you. We are called to put away all bitterness. If we don't put it away, we become the seeding source for this poisonous plant. Now, we become like weeds or villains that kill anything good. Therefore, if you want to eradicate this root of bitterness and its fruit from your life, it begins with identifying the source, forgiving this person, reconciling the relationship, and working on your heart by tilling it again to prepare it to receive the incorruptible seed of God's Word to produce good fruit.

When the battle against *bitterness* is seriously waged in our lives, there will be joy and freedom in our hearts that will replace the doom and gloom.

- Prayers will be answered because you're keeping the peace to keep the relationship intact.
- Breakthroughs will be realized because you're doing God's will to forgive to be forgiven.
- Silence will be broken because you can hear Him clearer now because your heart is right and ready to receive His directions.

When our hearts are right, we will experience liberation from the burden of bitterness, which ensnares us and deprives us of the abundant blessings God desires to bestow upon us for His glory. When our hearts are right, we will listen to sound counsel from God to become a voice of repentance, humility, and healing to ourselves as well as those people whom our poison has influenced by the *fruit of our bitterness*. If not, the *fruit of bitterness* in their life, which was outsourced from our bitterness, will continue to reproduce even though we are no longer in the equation.

Matthew 5:23-24 ESV
So if you are offering your gift at the altar and there, remember that your brother has something against you, leave your gift there before the altar and go. First be reconciled to your brother, and then come and offer your gift.

It's important to recognize that Jesus places a responsibility on us to take proactive steps in rectifying wrongs and participating in someone's healing if we have offended them. We are not to wait, but to go and do so quickly.

Testimony: God led me to do something extremely tough because I didn't have to do it much. I try my best not to hurt people because I don't like saying, "I'm Sorry." I know this isn't quite right, but it keeps me from deliberately hurting people. Now, don't get me wrong, I wasn't always saved, and I have hurt people, and I am very sorry for that. Anyway, I had to drop my pride and clothe myself in humility to ask someone to "forgive" me who I didn't think I had wronged, but because they felt I had, it was my duty as a mature Christian, a man of God, to make things right. Again, it's all about relationships, not who's right or wrong. We don't know how what we do makes someone feel.

We can't judge if their feelings are real or warranted. We can move based on what they tell us and then apologize to hopefully stop the seed of bitterness from taking root and later producing fruit. This person was hurt, but never talked to me about it. That seed of bitterness was growing unbeknownst to them and me. Because that seed of bitterness was not plucked up through effectively communicating about when it happened, it grew roots, and after some time, the fruits of bitterness started showing. I started hearing about how bad I was when I had been nothing but good to this person. It surprised me, but I knew exactly what it was when it reared its ugly head, and God showed me what needed to be done, but I didn't want to do it.

Nonetheless, I obeyed God because I love Him more than I love my feelings, and the relationship was amended. Unbeknownst to me, doors that were shut started to open and unanswered prayers were answered. See, when we focus on relationships by obeying God no matter how hard it may seem, asking for forgiveness when you don't feel you wrong someone, forgiving those who wrong us, and putting away bitterness, I am a witness that something powerful happens in the spiritual realm that causes breakthroughs in relationships, prayers, as well as our hearts.

Jesus is big on healthy relationships with Him, as well as with each other. He compels us to move closer and deeper into our relationship with Him, and He shows us how to destroy the *root of bitterness* to eliminate the fruit of bitterness. Not only will He show us how to find freedom, but He will also show us the victims of our bitterness who have not found freedom. He has given us a mission to clean up our mess, which is part of our recovery. If we do not humbly embrace this responsibility, we will continue to experience limitations to our recovery, and our *fruit of bitterness* in that person will continue.

Will you embrace your freedom and reach out to heal a broken or wounded relationship?

CHAPTER 14

LIFE BEYOND BITTERNESS IS LIBERATING

Philippians 4:13 NKJV
I can do all things through Christ who strengthens me.

Contrary to popular belief, we can do all things through Christ, who strengthens us because God said we can. So, as tough as it may seem, we can overcome heartbreak by smashing through the walls of hurt, pain, and betrayal that planted the seed of bitterness in our hearts to thrive in our relationships. Don't be discouraged by thinking you will always be miserable due to heartache and pain. We are free to live a life beyond bitterness.

In context, Paul was speaking about handling the lack and hardships that came along with his ministry. He could overcome all the adversity that came his way through Christ. And the same power that sustains us through hardships also enables us to do all things that the Lord leads us to do. We are not self-sufficient. And the Lord doesn't just do things for us. It's Christ working through us. We are partners with the Lord. Self-confidence is not of the Lord. All our ability in the Christian life is found in Christ. It is not our ability that makes us strong but our availability through Christ that enables us.

2 Corinthians 12:10 NKJV
Therefore I take pleasure in infirmities, in reproaches, in needs, in persecutions, in distresses, for Christ's sake. For when I am weak, then I am strong.

This Bible scripture tells us that when we recognize our inability to deal with tough things like bitterness, we need to rely on the Lord, and then the Lord's strength will flow through us to make us more than conquered over the hurt, pain, and trauma that caused the bitterness. This is how we can do all things through Christ who strengthens us.

You can survive any storm in your relationship if you do not eat the forbidden fruit of bitterness that will destroy everything you've established. We can defeat bitterness if we give it to God. We don't have to be trapped in a hopeless place of damning and demoralizing bitterness. People will say and do hurtful things that we can't control, but we can control how we handle it, which is very important. So, stop complaining, or you will remain in it. It's our responsibility to cast our cares upon the Lord because He cares enough for us to give us the strength to forgive and get over it.

Now, as with anything we deal with, we must recognize and acknowledge that it exists because if we deny it, we will remain a slave to it and never receive our freedom from it. I have met so many that are well put together on the inside, but miserable on the inside. They are secretly drowning in depression, anxiety, shame, low self-esteem, trust issues, abandonment, loneliness, and a host of other self-inflicted issues and don't know how to get rid of them. They try on their own, but after some time, they go right back to feeling and behaving the same way because they only tried to deal with the outer without addressing the inner or root of the issue. If you ask most people with forgiveness problems, trust issues, anger, addictive personalities, fear, and even depression if they are bitter about something or someone, they will probably tell you no, simply because they don't know what bitterness is. Bitterness, at its simplest meaning, is anger and disappointment at being treated unfairly. It's synonymous with resentment and envy or jealousy. It can be any secondary emotions, stemming from insult, injury, or even bullying. Unrealized to its victims, bitterness can be caused by being hurt, disappointment, unkind/hurtful words, unjust treatment, and unmet expectations, to name a few, such as when a parent tells a child that they are going to do something over and over again and never do it, a spouse that verbally abuses their spouse or children, friends that cheat with their friends' mates, people that tell you one thing and do another. This is usually the onset of bitterness.

Three phases of bitterness progressively get worse if not properly dealt with:

- Phase 1: The Seed of Bitterness - planted by the negative actions of others.

- Phase 2: The Root of Bitterness – inward emotions that grow when watered by the constant rehearsal of other's negative actions.

- Phase 3: The Fruit of Bitterness – outward negative actions produced from the seed that grew roots that are now so strong that they affect you and your relationships.

This is a deadly and vicious disease that kills, steals, and destroys, just like the enemy of our souls does. Depending on the phase of bitterness you find yourself in, it will require different steps to rid yourself of this detrimental and demoralizing pestilence.

Phase 1 - The Seed of Bitterness:

1. Acknowledge Bitterness Existence
2. Be Liberated by Casting Bitterness On God
3. Forgive Not Forget to Thrive
4. Banish Bitterness by Putting it Away

When the Seed of Bitterness is planted, we must acknowledge its' existence. Bitterness is from the pit of hell, and the biggest deception the devil plays on humanity is to try to make us think he and hell don't exist. So, to start digging up the seed of bitterness before it can set root is to acknowledge the hurt, disappointment, and unmet expectations. Remembering and acknowledging, them may be painful, but it's necessary to cast them on God, who can handle everything we cannot.

We cannot defeat bitterness if we do not give it to God! We cannot always control what happens to us, but we can control how we react and what we do with it. We can choose to try to handle it on our own and lose, or we can choose to give it to God and win every time. So, instead of grumbling and complaining about your bitter situations or worse, ignoring they exist, God invites us to verbalize the offense in the safety of His presence because He is there to help, uphold, strengthen us to forgive and do what's necessary to become the victor and not the victim.

Because we are forgiven, we can forgive, which is one of our reasonable services. To defeat bitterness in this first phase, we must be willing to forgive those who hurt us because it frees us from the grip of bitterness. Remember and never forget that forgiveness is not for them; it's for us because they will never ask for it in most cases. However, just because we forgive doesn't mean we need to forget. Those memories are there to keep us safe. They remind us of what to do along with what not to do.

Conversely, just because we remember what they did doesn't mean we must rehearse what they did. We must put it away by not recounting and rehearsing it all the time. If we don't put away all bitterness, which is a silent sin, it will continue to break up relationships, and break down our ability to find freedom, peace, and rest in our hearts that will usher us into the next phase.

Phase 2 - The Root of Bitterness:

1. Protect Your Heart
2. Live In Peace
3. Look After Each Other

Protecting our hearts from the sting and bite of bitterness is vital. We must protect our hearts from this poisonous venom of bitterness at all costs because our behavior flows out of a fully functioning heart, or inner person. What comes out of a person defiles a person. This is one reason they say that hurting people hurts people. So, let's make sure we properly deal with hurt as instructed in Phase 1 in order not to hurt others, which is outside of God's will. Let's drop our pride and lean on God to help heal our broken hearts so we can live in peace with one another.

As Christians, it is our calling to live in peace with everyone. Peace must be at the forefront of our agenda. Peace is the secret ingredient to guarding our hearts and minds through Christ Jesus. He preached in the beatitudes in Matthew 5:9, *"Blessed are the peacemakers, for they will be called children of God."* Nothing should supersede our desire to be children of God.

Also, understand that keeping the peace or being meek doesn't make you weak. Being meek is having power without power having you. Jesus was the meekest person to walk the earth. Being meek is simply power under control. In essence, you possess the ability to harbor resentment, anger, and frustration towards those who have wronged you, but you opt not to do so to maintain peace. This demonstrates your meekness, which will ultimately guide you towards God's blessings because you have chosen to obey Him by caring for His children.

We must look out for each other and not let bitterness blow out the candle of our peace, happiness, and joy to leave our souls in bitter darkness. People are going to do what they do, and there is nothing we can do about it. If someone tells you who they are by hurting you, believe them, forgive them, walk in peace with them, and look out for them to receive grace from God to protect your heart and put all bitterness away so that it will not take root to trouble you and defile and corrupt others. If we don't do these things because of our stubbornness or just our inability to, we will find ourselves in the deadliest, but not unresolvable phase.

Phase 3 - The Forbidden Fruit of Bitterness:

1. Relationship-Minded
2. Reconciliation-Focused
3. Right Heart-Created

If you have reached Phase 3, that means you didn't catch bitterness in time and are now reaping the forbidden fruit of Bitterness, where your relationships are affected more and more due to your actions. You are saying and doing things that are dividing and separating you from others instead of bringing you together. The very essence of our existence hinges on relationships, which cannot flourish unless we are united.

Think about this briefly to understand how important relationships are to our Father. God sent Jesus to earth to reestablish our relationship with Him. But, instead of accepting Him, mankind crucified Him, but our loving God was still willing to lay down His life to reconcile the relationship. We must be relationship-minded! God looks past all the hurt and pain we still cause Him today to have a relationship with us.

He has every right to be bitter because we fail to meet His standards, but He doesn't because the relationship is more important than anything else. We should always strive to walk in God's kind of love characterized by putting others ahead of self (Philippians 2:3). According to Jesus, the greatest expression of self-sacrifice for others is laying down one's life, to reconcile or bring together for a relationship.

Reconciliation basically means to restore relationships like Jesus restored or reconciled our relationship with the Father through the atonement or payment of our sins with His perfect and sinless life. The key to reconciliation is going through the above steps in every stage to effectively deal with the root cause of the animosity, dislike, ill will, hatred, and hostility that has caused a dispute and separation between people.

When bitterness takes root, it produces fruit that will wound and poison anyone who tastes it. The fruit we are supposed to produce comes from our abiding relationship with Jesus that imparts the Holy Spirit in us, which dwells His fruits of love, joy, peace, patience, kindness, goodness, faithfulness, gentleness, and self-control (Galatians 5:22). When we walk as Jesus walked, we are bound to reap the fruit of His ministry and message of forgiveness to bless us with the ministry of reconciliation. That doesn't mean we must like and accept everything people do, but we must walk in love to live peaceably with them. This is not easy, and that is why we need Jesus leading us to walk after the Spirit, not to fulfill the lust of the flesh, where bitterness lives to give an eye for an eye and a tooth for a tooth.

This is our sinful nature and how we naturally respond. This is why the Lord has created in us clean hearts and put new spirits within us at salvation. When someone tries to dig up the root of bitterness in their life, their heart or the soil of their heart must be improved. There is nothing good that can come from bitterness. When our hearts are right, we will listen to sound counsel from God. Our Lord and Savior makes Himself present, holding out His nail-pierced hand, and extending His strong arm of redemption to reconcile us to the Father so that we can reconcile with one another through the hurt and pain that causes bitterness.

The Word of God and the gospel of Jesus Christ can free us and truly help us Overcome Life's Greatest Pains that can lead to bitterness. We must remain focused on relationships instead of retaliation and reconciliation instead of separation, just like Jesus did. This will create in us a right heart in God. I know your hearts have been broken so badly that you don't even believe it can be healed to reconcile relationships through forgiving those who hurt you. Well, the good news is, the Lord has created in us clean hearts and put new spirits within us at salvation (Psalms 51:10). Now, you can do all things through Christ who strengthens you (Philippians 4:13). You can't do it on your own, but you can do it with Him.

So, when someone hurts you and lets you down, don't harbor it; acknowledge it immediately to cast it on the Lord because He cares for you. Forgive them and put that pain away for your sake, not necessarily theirs. Move on by asking God to protect your heart to help you live in peace and look after your fellow brothers and sisters to not hurt them in the way you've been hurt. Remember, relationship, not retaliation, is God's portion for us. Therefore, when you've done all that you can do to reconcile those godly relationships, remember all can't be reconciled; you will have a right heart because you know in your heart of hearts that you did what God has instructed you to do to defeat bitterness and prevent others from eating its' forbidden fruit.

As I conclude this book, let me encourage you, for your sake and the sake of others, to make the right moves to remove bitterness from your heart now instead of later. You must acknowledge your bitterness and initiate the process to rid yourself of it. You can start by reaching out to those people you know you hurt due to the bitterness in your heart caused by them or someone else and ask them to forgive you for the wrong that you did to them. It's not about what they did to you; it's all about what you did or may have done to them. This will remove the burden of heaviness from you and free them from the seed of bitterness that you planted that may be producing fruit in their lives. Lean on the Lord, pursue peace by any means necessary because the fruit of the Spirit will destroy every fruit of bitterness to help you as well as others Overcome Life's Greatest pains that produce Life's Greatest fruit of bitterness.

Embrace your liberation from the shackles of bitterness that have burdened you for far too long. As you cast off the weight of resentment and unforgiveness, step boldly into the bound-less realm of newfound freedom. Victory over the forbidden fruit of bitterness is within your grasp. Prepare to savor the exquisite sweetness of freedom after the bitterness of pain. It's time to taste and see the abundant joys that await on the other side of healing. Take action now and unlock the door to a future brimming with love, peace, and boundless possibilities.

ABOUT THE AUTHOR

Shawn Turner is the senior pastor of Faith-Hope & Love Christian Church (FHLCC) in Mableton, Georgia. Through dynamic Sunday online services and a global Bible Study By Phone, Shawn delivers the Word of God with clarity and relevance, empowering listeners to apply it in their daily lives.

With over 25 years of ordained ministry experience, Shawn specializes in preaching and teaching God's Word, officiating marriages, and offering premarital counseling and marital coaching. Before this book, Shawn authored "If Only I Knew Before I Said I Do" and "How To Keep The Flames Burning." Alongside his wife Yolanda, who married in 1996, Shawn is a dedicated father to three daughters, grandfather to one grandson, and Godfather to many.

Explore Pastor Shawn's transformative ministry and discover profound insights for living a life rooted in faith, hope, and love at either of the following websites:

Ministry: www.shawnturnerministries.com
Church: www.fhlccltd.com
YouTube: www.youtube.com/@faith-hope-love-cc

CALL TO ACTION

I help **Frustrated** and **Stagnant** couples that are fighting and not getting along overcome **Ineffective Communication** so that they can become a **POWER COUPLE** and experience lasting **Love**, **Joy**, and **Intimacy** in **God's Way**.

Shawn Turner
Pastor/Author/Relationship Coach

If your relationship is experiencing:

- **Hurt/Pain/Bitterness**
- **Infidelity**
- **Ineffective Communication**
- **Lack of Intimacy**
- **Financial Issues**
- **Unrealistic Expectations**
- **Unforgiveness**
- **Undefined Marital Roles**
- **Loneliness**
- **And a Host of Other Marital Issues**

Get the necessary wisdom, knowledge, and understanding to get you from where you are to where God ordained you to be.

Hosea 4:6 NKJV
My people are destroyed for lack of knowledge...

You can't change that which you don't confront, and you can't confront that which you don't know. If you continue doing the same thing, you will continue receiving the same results. So, take charge of your future by deciding to do something about it today. You've taken the first step by purchasing this book, and as my thank you:

Claim Your Free 1-On-1 Breakthrough Strategy Session:
(Choose One of the Following Ways)

Website: www.shawnturnerministries.com or www.fhlccltd.com
(Download Free Gift)

Facebook: https://www.facebook.com/sturner04/ (Direct Message Me)

Email: pastor@shawnturnerministries.com or sturner@fhlccltd.com

Provide name, number, email and Free 1:1 Breakthrough Strategy Session in Subject Line

www.ingramcontent.com/pod-product-compliance
Lightning Source LLC
Chambersburg PA
CBHW060323130626
46553CB00003B/901